LA FOLK TALES

JENNIE BAILEY &
DAVID ENGLAND

The
History
Press

First published 2014

The History Press
The Mill, Brimscombe Port
Stroud, Gloucestershire, GL5 2QG
www.thehistorypress.co.uk

British Library Cataloguing in Publication Data.
A catalogue record for this book is available from the British Library.

ISBN 978 0 7524 8993 3

Typesetting and origination by The History Press
Printed in Great Britain

CONTENTS

ABOUT THE AUTHORS AND ARTISTS

AUTHORS

Jennie Bailey

Jennie is a prize-winning writer and self-confessed 'word nerd'. She writes fiction, plays, articles and poetry. Her writing is inspired by nature – walking, being in nature, and the changes of the seasons. Although she lives in Greater Manchester, she is constantly dazzled by pockets of wildlife that appear in the most urban places.

Jennie believes that anyone can tell stories, and she supports children and adults in exploring and developing writing skills.

She has poetry published in various anthologies and has written and directed plays with the Didsbury Players, a Manchester drama group. *Lancashire Folk Tales* is her first collaborative book.

Her website is www.jenbee.me.uk.

David England

David is a man of many parts: writer, storyteller, psychotherapist and shamanic guide – not separate parts so much as different aspects which interconnect and interact together.

David says, 'I love telling stories which make me laugh. Stories which I know can captivate an audience. Stories which touch the soul.' He loves writing stories just the same way. For him, storytelling is a dialogue with the audience, and as a writer he seeks dialogue with a wider audience. His book *Berkshire Folk Tales*, with researcher-supreme and co-author Tina Bilbé, was published by The History Press in 2013.

His storytelling website is davidengland.co.uk.

ARTISTS

Jo Lowes

Jo is a freelance photographer / graphic artist and teacher at Salford College, Greater Manchester. Her inspiration comes from travelling, two pesky cats, doodling and making sure her camera never leaves her side. More work can be seen at sheshouldbequiet.wordpress.com. For more info contact Joesylowesy@hotmail.com.

Adelina Pintea

Having worked in interior design, Adelina has always been an addict of the Rotring art pen and the uncanny watercolour washes that give it life. Originally from Transylvania, she is now Manchester-based with a portfolio that features urban sketches, the nonspeaking world of animals and scripted stories. Her website is www.adelinapintea.co.uk.

ACKNOWLEDGEMENTS

The authors should like to thank The History Press commissioning editors Nicola Guy and Declan Flynn, as well as Helen Bradbury and Ross Britton from marketing, and especially Chris Ogle for his helpful and responsive approach to his editorial work.

A thank you to all the writers and storytellers of the nine-teenth and twentieth centuries for collecting and recording such a wealth of folk tales, especially Frank Hird, John Harland & T.T. Wilkinson, Revd Thomas Cruddas Porteus and John Roby.

David should like to thank his family and friends for their patient support, especially his son Ed for his editing work, and his friends for listening to his stories, in particular Sylvia Friend, Jane Morrell and Simon Smith. Thanks also to Slough Writers for the invaluable contact with other professional writers, and especially to chairman Terry Adlam for his consistent support. His local librarian, Derek Beaven, a brilliant writer of literary fiction, for his support and encouragement, and to all who have helped along the way: Sir Bernard de Hoghton of Hoghton Tower; Revd Ray Hutchinson, rector of the parish church of All Saints, Wigan; the church cleaning team at St Elphin's church, Warrington; and to the security guard who showed us the dungeon in Lancaster Castle where the Pendle witches had been incarcerated.

Jennie should like to thank her family and friends; Bury Heritage Library; Rebecca Daker; Tom Goodale; Richard Goulding; Dr Simon Heywood; Sarah Hau; Rob Hawley (and Jonas!); Dr Graham Kemp; Lancashire County Council; Lancaster Castle; Manchester Metropolitan University; Middleton Library; the People's History Museum; the Portico Library; Dr John Sears; Touchstones Local Studies Centre (especially for showing her their 'Weird and Wonderful' files) and James Young.

1

Welcome!

Welcome to *Lancashire Folk Tales*! My name is Lily Battersby and this is my friend and fellow storyteller, Dr Fred Hibbert. This evening we shall take you on a magical, mystery tour of old Lancashire, telling folk tales as we go.

We'll be poking around haunted houses, bumping into boggarts, seeing how many clever Lancashire folk trick the Devil. There will be witches, a giant, a dragon and we will try to avoid the wicked Jinny Greenteeth!

As time is malleable, we will be travelling by various miraculous means – many of which can no longer be travelled on. From the transporter bridge and swing aqueduct to horse and carriage over Morecambe's sands, we'll take you on a journey around the wonderful County Palatine of Lancashire.

Let's tarry no longer – mount up and let's be off!

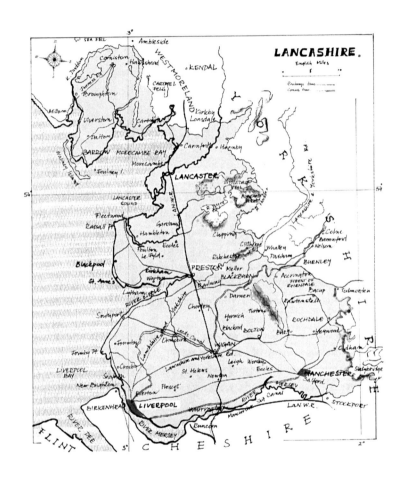

2

THE PHANTOM VOICE, SOUTHPORT

LILY: This story could be from anywhere along the golden coast of the north-west, however, it was retold in Southport by John Roby, and it is to Southport where we all arrive on horseback, from the south, the north, the east, or mysteriously cantering over the sands from the west.

We leave our horses to graze a grassy patch on Marine Drive then take the smart Southport Pier Tramway car the 1,216-yard trip over the sands to the end of the pier. Here Fred will tell us this chilling tale from these rose gold sands, the Phantom Voice.

❧

The expansive coastline of Southport stretches for miles before you see the waves of the Irish Sea. The town itself, once a great resort, still has impressive natural surroundings. There's the sharp tang of fish and chips in the air, and grand, brick houses are wrought with fancy ironwork.

But long ago, before Southport was a bustling holiday destination, there lived Bridget, who was the venerable, if eccentric, landlady of a local ale house. This pub was a moribund establishment, the only warmth and comfort coming from its blazing fires. The men came in to drink and contemplate the hardness of life. Around the well-lit bar area were twenty-one buxom brass mermaids. Fashioned to look the same, the aquatic sisters were sculpted, lounging back with one hand forever playing with long bronzed hair. These metallic sirens were supposed to represent several unfortunate souls who had lost their lives in a tragic sea accident. Bridget was known locally as a seer: one who could look into the future.

Who knew what she said about the fantastical goings on in her pub the night a young man came in with fear in his eyes, shivering and shaking like a thistle in the wind. The majority of the drinkers remembered that night for years, and the story passed into legend; the events of that evening engraved on their very souls. Many drank to try to forget it. Many drank to blot out the memories of the perils wrought along the barren tract of golden sand.

The current of the Irish Sea hits the water from the mouths of two mighty rivers, the Ribble and, further south, the Mersey. Shipwrecks were frequent in the area; nearly one hundred vessels had been wrecked within the last few decades, and especially at night when the sea mist was at its zenith.

It had been an unusually bright October day, the sort of warm autumnal weather that leads to a bone cold evening. The stars shone like polished pieces of bone. This was when a young man burst into the pub with wild eyes and an icy sweat on his brow. Bridget's usual clientèle beheld him with silence, suspicion, and narrowed eyes. Even the usually smiling Bridget, her hankerings aside, momentarily ceased polishing the tankards.

The young man had been travelling on horseback along the sand dunes of the perilous coastal track of the oversands. His journey had led him from the north, over Morecambe Bay. Bridget, feeling slightly sorry for the lad, gave him a pint of beer and entreated him to repeat his tale to the now curious crowd …

I've travelled in on horseback, and I've not seen my steed for hours. Not since I found the horror on the shore. The night seems to fall faster in the north and I was soon lost in what seemed like a labyrinth of fern and sand. My route seemed circular and there appeared to be no discerning beacon nor object to direct me. My horse had slowed to a ramble and slowly picked his way through the succession of monotonous rising and falling dunes.

From the valley of sand I could barely see the stars and had a feeling that the low moan of the sea was portentous. I feared that my horse and I may be lost by a quick shift in the tide and my journey south would end in this unknown town.

This dread overtook my steed, and he stopped and stood stock-still. There was no sound save for the rush, the push of the sea. I dismounted and swear that the shifting sands made demonic patterns. I thought I heard a rustle and held my hand up to my ear to amplify the sound. But there was nothing; all I felt was my wet fringe, salted to my head. I tried to pull the horse along but he was having none of it. I feared he was an animal possessed; there was no moving him with sharp tugs on his bridle. I dismounted him and tried to lead him along.

Now, beyond the sea's boom, I distinctly heard a sound. Maybe a fisherman out late, or perhaps another man with a need to be out at this hour?   But there was terror in that voice that affected my senses too.

At intervals I made out a low, rasping voice, a voice which sounded like it bubbled in blood: 'Murder! Murder!' was the only thing this voice uttered, but in such agony that I had never heard before – like a voice from beyond the grave.

I clung to my horse, taking small relief in the heat from the blood of the animal. But the voice was getting louder, closer, more urgent. I thought that it was the end; that Death himself had come to claim me, or worse, some other diabolical fiend, the Devil himself. For I have heard tales of the Devil's many dealings in Lancashire.

'Murder! Murder!' the voice repeated. I steeled myself; if I was to deal with Satan then I would do so with bravery and spirit in my heart.

Then, all of a sudden, I smelled and felt the rotten, clammy breath of one whom was no longer of this earth. I cried out, 'What in the name of...?!' Then there was a crash as if a body had fallen in front of me.

Although it shames me now, I have to admit that I closed my eyes and fell to my knees. I felt my horse bolt, the bridle slipping from my fingers. I crouched down, with eyes still firmly shut, and felt around me. I stretched out my hand and my fingers brushed something. I felt further forward and my hand rested on the cold face of a corpse. Where his eyes had been I felt a slimy trail.

I screamed – I entreat you that any other grown man would do the same – felt the blood rush to my head and heart. It was here that I fainted beside this abomination.

I have no idea how long I was out cold for. I woke in the hope that it was a dream, and that I was safe in the boarding house near Silverdale. But no, I was on chilled sand with the dead man. Once roused, I made out the features of the man – bloodstains silvered by the sliver of a quarter moon – and I ran up the first track I found.

I followed this track at speed and it brought me here. Seeing the friendly fire and hearing this pub's merriment I felt that I would be safe to retell my tale.

The men and Bridget listened entranced, horrified by this macabre story. Some men laughed; they did not believe him. The young man then stared wildly around the room, 'If anyone is man enough to come with me, I will show you where this poor wretch lies.'

Every eye was on the lad, some suspicious, some afraid. There was the unspoken agreement that if there was a body out there then the least it deserved was a proper burial, not to be left to the sport of foxes and marauding gulls.

Some of the men goaded each other, the scared looks palpable in some eyes. Some spoke loudly that the young man had probably encountered a boggart, or that perhaps he had partaken in flights of fancy so popular in pulp fiction.

There was a clanging noise. It was Kate, the teenage daughter of Bridget, who was taking down a lantern.

'Yer nowt but a big bunch of cowards, shame on thee. I be gang down there, with this 'ere young lad, follow me if yer dare.'

With her cloak and slightly dilapidated lantern, Kate had shamed the assorted audience into action. Kate's sweetheart, a sailor, manfully took his woman by her arm. She shook him off, she was nobody's prize. Thus the crowd grew into a sizeable search party.

At the front of this strange, slightly inebriated party was the young man, Kate and her beau. Other men lurked behind, each trying to bolster the courage of his neighbour. They made their way in near silence, the young man narrowed his eyes in order to get used to the weak light from Kate's lantern.

A dark movement elicited a sudden heart-stopping scream from the back of the crowd. Fortunately, it was nothing but a fine, chestnut horse: the young man's mount. The young man was so pleased at being reacquainted with his friend that he stumbled over the moss of a dune and nearly trod on the torso of the crowd's gory quarry: the body of the dead man.

Kate's paramour was violently sick when he beheld the twisted features of the man, his eyes removed as if by the force of a blunt object. His final moments must have been of such agony, of such degradation. The young man threw his cloak over the body, and shivering, entreated the others to assist with moving the body back to Bridget's tavern. Kate led the way back and this time, the strange procession was fully silent. It seemed that not even the tide would disrespect the quiet.

Upon returning to the pub, the body was laid upon a pallet in the outhouse. The young man was put to bed by Bridget and made as if to sleep. By now it was past midnight, and the young man could not sleep, his mind was troubled by the outcome of that violent crime. Although he had not witnessed how the poor man had been murdered, he felt moved to discover more.

As Bridget was closing up for the night, a violent storm raged. It was as if the weather wanted to have closure on this crime. The young man heard the meagre outhouse creak and groan, expecting that any second it would collapse on its poor inhabitant. The young man roused himself from his bed, the night making his quarters blacker than the soul of Old Nick himself. The sonorous sound of the rising tempest seemed to shake the pub, threatening to reduce the building back to its foundations.

Making his way back into the main body of the pub, the young man found Bridget and her daughter Kate clutched together, terrified. The fire in the hearth was dwindling, and Bridget was staring into it, lost in her mad ministries. Bridget gibbered and rocked as her daughter sat still and silently besides her. Kate said, 'Me mother is a seer; she's seen omens from the sea. She listens to the music of the dark, she 'eard the dead man sing a song of murder.'

As if in agreement, Bridget moaned as the waves crashed something weighty upon the shore.

'It's there, again, again! Poor wretch aboard, drop into the water with your death yell.' Bridget cried.

Both the young man and Kate made to the window and beheld a small vessel bobbing violently on the surface of the swell. It was now that the storm died down, and both the maid and the young man, in unspoken agreement, made to prepare out to see if they could save a life, even though one had already been lost that night. Kate grabbed the horn lamp once more and they left the quivering Bridget to her under-breath mutterings.

They ran back towards the beach, stumbling, slipping and sinking in the wet sand, back down the track near where the body was discovered. They heard a crowd by the shore, and by the dim light of the horn made out that some of the voices came from the denizens of the pub now sobered and ready for action. The clouds knotted above them like a furrowed brow, and there between the light of the moon and Kate's horn lamp, the outline of a small wrecked ship was discernible. A pencil sketch on slate.

The forms of the crowd were men and women, fishermen, the pub drinkers, all from the local community perhaps showing spirit in rescuing the boat's single inhabitant. Or perhaps there for plundering from under the protesting, last gasps of its owner.

And there he was, gasping like a fish in air. He looked as if he belonged to the sea and the crowd had stolen him from it. He looked exhausted, his eyes bloodshot and wild. He was half-carried, half-dragged by the young man and a couple of assembled crowd members. The crowd went to rip the boat apart grabbing what they could from it, like carrion to an old kill.

The lucky sailor was taken to the pub where Bridget warily gave him a pint of strong spirits to revive him. The man groaned deeply as he retold his tale, 'I'm nearly done in, all me crew are gone to

Davy Jones. As I saw the crew go down I tied mesel' to a jib. But I'm knackered as now, and need me rest. I'll tell thee more in t'morn.'

The only space in the small pub where the guest could comfortably sleep was next to the corpse in the outhouse. Feeling that the sea captain would not mind so quiet a companion, Kate lead on to his berth.

The captain was not best pleased at the concept of passing the night with a corpse; it seemed like the least unpleasant alternative (that being in the smelly stables with the horses). He was assisted to his chamber where they would help move the corpse from the pallet to change occupants so he may pass the night in a more comfortable manner.

He was helped up to his rude bed. Then he let out a piercing and terrible shriek. The captain sat bolt upright next to the corpse, his eyeballs protruding where the corpse's did not, his face set in mortal dread. While expecting the bravest of men to be fearful of the dead man, this was something altogether different. The captain's eyes were fixed on the dead man as if in cold recognition.

'I know that man. Aye! Indeed I do; yesterday he were at t'helm of boat. Long has he bin insubordinate and long have I born him a grudge. I plotted revenge I did. Late last afternoon we were alone on deck and 'e lunged. I aimed a blow. Knocked 'im clean out. I plunged a nearby boat hook into his hateful eyes and pushed him o'erboard. As I did, I heard a moan, it struck me deeply like tolling of a dull bell, that word: MURDER! I swear I heard it now! Jus' as I lifted 'is shroud!'

With this confession, there was nothing else for it; he himself admitted he had little left to live for. In the morning, justice came for the captain and he was put to death for the crime that he took brief, bitter-sweet pleasure in committing.

LILY: Still trembling from the story, we return to our horses and canter through the flat, fertile horticultural landscape to the magnificent Wetland Centre at Martin Mere. We spread a tarpaulin by the banks of Martin Mere, at the time of our next story the largest body of fresh water in England, and sit to hear a tale of Sir Lancelot du Lac.

3

SIR LANCELOT
AND SIR TARQUIN,
MARTIN MERE

FRED: Sir Lancelot, you may be surprised to hear, has a close association with the county. 'Lanc' is the Celtic term for a spear, and 'lot' refers to the people of the land, hence 'Lancelot's shire' or as it is known today 'Lancashire'. Lily will tell his tale …

In the turbulent times following the Roman withdrawal, marauding bands laid waste the land and its people, until King Arthur emerged as a commanding leader to fill the power vacuum and subdue the marauders.

In the north, the remnant of British knights invited the Saxons to help repulse the violent incursions of Picts and Scots, but the perfidious Saxons appropriated the land for themselves and turned the British knights out of their castles.

The greatest, cruellest and most treacherous of the Saxon knights was Sir Tarquin, who dwelt in a castle of great strength, which he had gained by treachery from a British knight. The castle was surrounded by vast ramparts, flanked by high and stately towers. Sir Tarquin was a knight of brutal aspect, gigantic stature and prodigious strength. It is so fabled that each day for his morning repast he devoured an infant child, its little legs still thrashing as they slid between his pitiless lips.

To contend with the marauding bands, and later the usurping Saxons, King Arthur commissioned a force of brave knights, spearheaded by his Knights of the Round Table, foremost of whom was named Sir Lancelot du Lac.

As an infant, Lancelot had been overlooked by his mother Queen Helen while she cradled her dying husband King Ban of Benoit in her arms. King Ban lay dying of grief to see his besieged, beloved castle in flames.

With the far-sightedness given by living his life backwards, Merlin the Magician knew there was a time of terror and turmoil to come. He conjured deep and powerful magic to prepare the land for this time, aided by his mistress, the nymph Viviane.

With Queen Helen despairing and distracted, Viviane spirited the infant Lancelot away and bore him over the seas to the deep, wide waters of Martin Mere, and down into its fabulous subterraneous caverns, where she held her court. There she raised him, tutoring him to be the finest, bravest knight in all the land, against the chaotic and tumultuous times to come. At the age of eighteen she raised him from the waters of the lake and presented him at the court of King Arthur.

The young warrior quickly proved his mettle and was invested with the badge of knighthood. His person, prowess, and unparalleled gallantry won the heart of many a fair damsel in this splendid abode of chivalry and romance. He was acknowledged as the finest, bravest knight in all the land, and fulfilled his prophetic name Lancelot du Lac, ruler of Lancelot's shire, the one who had emerged from the lake of Martin Mere, to face this time of trial.

In the bloody war between King Arthur's knights and the Saxons, the country was ravaged by fire and sword, and many puissant knights were slain or incarcerated. Sir Tarquin boasted of no mean success – he had threescore and four British knights held in thrall, chained to the walls of his deepest, darkest dungeon.

Sir Lancelot du Lac was at Shrewsbury's fair town, in mortal combat with Sir Carados, a ferocious giant of a Saxon knight and brother to Sir Tarquin. After seven hours of battle, Lancelot hewed

Carados down like a blasted elm. Lancelot, casting himself upon the ground exhausted, was carried from thence by enchantment, and on waking found himself in an unknown forest, where he sojourned a while.

At the forest edge was a vast trackless wilderness, devoid of birdsong or habitation, where he saw a damsel of such inexpressible and ravishing beauty that none might behold her without the most heart-stirring delight and admiration. To this maiden did Sir Lancelot address himself, but she hid her face and fell a-weeping. He then enquired the cause of her dolour, when she bade him flee, for his life was in great jeopardy.

'Oh, Sir Knight!' uncovering her face as she spoke, 'The giant Tarquin, who liveth hereabout, like the dragon of yore entailed a desert round his dwelling. So fierce and rapacious is he that no man durst live beside him, save that he hold his life and property of too mean account, and too worthless for the taking. Thou wert as good as dead should he espy thee so near his castle. Flee! Flee!'

Lancelot had heard of how this Sir Tarquin was playing the eagle in its eyrie amongst his companions and brethren of the Round Table: gaining from the powerful and the wealthy, and watching and biding his time before an attack.

'What!' said the knight, 'and shall Sir Lancelot du Lac flee before this false and cruel tyrant? To this purpose am I come, that I may slay and make an end of him at once, and deliver the captive knights from his dungeon.'

'Art thou, indeed, Sir Lancelot?' said the damsel, joy suddenly starting through her tears, 'Then is our deliverance nearer than we dared hope. Thy fame is gone before thee into all lands, and thy might and thy prowess none may withstand. This evil one, Sir Tarquin, hath taken captive many a true knight who betook himself to this adventure, and now lieth in chains and foul ignominy, without hope of release, till death break off his fetters.'

'Beshrew me,' said Lancelot, 'but I will deliver them presently, and cut off the foul tyrant's head, or lose mine own by the attempt.'

He followed the maiden to a river's brink, near to where, as tradition still reports, Knott Mill now stands. Having mounted her upon his steed, she pointed out a path over the ford, beyond which he soon espied the castle, a vast and stately building of rugged stone, like a huge crown upon the hilltop, presenting a gentle ascent from the stream.

Now did Sir Lancelot alight, as well to assist his companion as to bethink himself what course to pursue. However, the damsel showed him a high tree, about a stone's throw from the ditch before the castle, whereon hung a goodly array of accoutrements, with many fine and costly shields, on which were displayed a variety of fair and fanciful devices, the property of the knights then held in durance by Sir Tarquin. Below them all hung a copper basin, on which was carved the inscription: 'Who valueth not his life a whit, Let him this magic basin hit.'

This so enraged Sir Lancelot that he drove at the vessel violently with his spear, piercing it through and through, so vigorous was the assault. The clangour was loud, and anxiously did the knight await some reply to his summons. Yet there was no answer, nor was there any stir about the walls or outworks. It seemed as though Sir Tarquin was his own castellan, skulking there alone, like the cunning spider watching for his prey.

Silence, with her vast, unmoving wings, appeared to brood over the place, and the echo, which gave back their summons from the walls, seemed to labour for utterance through the void by which they were encompassed – a stillness so appalling might needs discourage the hot and fiery purpose of Sir Lancelot. But this knight, unused but to the rude clash of arms and the mêlée of battle, did marvel exceedingly at the forbearance of the enemy.

Yet he still rode round about the fortress, expecting that someone should come forth to inquire his business, and this he did, to and fro, for a long space. As he was just minded to return from so fruitless an adventure, he saw a cloud of dust at some distance, and presently he beheld a knight galloping furiously towards him. Coming nigh, Sir Lancelot was aware that a captive knight lay before him, bound hand and foot, bleeding and sore wounded.

'Villain!' cried Sir Lancelot, 'and unworthy the name of a true and loyal knight, how darest thou do this insult and contumely to an enemy, who, though fallen, is yet thine equal! I will make thee rue this foul despite, and avenge the wrongs of my brethren of the Round Table.'

'If thou be for so brave a meal,' said Tarquin, 'thou shalt have thy fill, and that speedily. I shall first cut off thy head, and then serve up thy carcase to the Round Table, for both that and thee I do utterly defy!'

'This is over-dainty food for thy sending,' replied Sir Lancelot hastily, and with that they couched their spears.

The first rush was over, but man and horse had withstood the shock. Again they fell back, measuring the distance with an eager and impetuous glance, and again they rushed on, as if to overwhelm each other by main strength, when, as fortune would have it, their lances shivered, both of them at once, in the rebound. The end of Sir Lancelot's spear, as it broke, struck his adversary's steed on the shoulder, and caused him to fall suddenly, as if sore wounded. Sir Tarquin leaped nimbly from off his back, which Sir Lancelot espying, cried out, 'Now will I show thee proper courtesy, for, by mine honour and the faith of a true knight, I shall not slay thee at this foul advantage.'

Alighting with haste, they betook themselves to their swords, each guarding the opposite attack warily with his shield. That of Sir Tarquin was framed of a bull's hide, stoutly held together with thongs and, in truth, seemed well-nigh impenetrable, whilst the shield of his opponent, being of more brittle stuff, did seem as though it would have cloven asunder with the desperate strokes of Sir Tarquin's sword.

Nothing daunted, Sir Lancelot broke ofttimes through his adversary's guard and smote him once until his blood gushed forth. At this sight, Sir Tarquin waxed ten times more fierce, and summoning all his strength for the blow, wrought so lustily on the head of Sir Lancelot that he began to reel, which Tarquin observed, by a side blow struck the sword from out his hand, with so sharp and dexterous a jerk that it shivered into a thousand fragments.

'Now yield thee, Sir Knight, or thou diest,' and with that the cruel monster sprang upon him to accomplish his end. Still Sir Lancelot would not yield, nor sue to him for quarter, but flew on his enemy like the ravening wolf to his prey. Then were they seen hurtling together like wild bulls, Sir Lancelot holding fast his adversary's sword, so that in vain he attempted to make a thrust therewith.

'Thou discourteous churl! Give me but the vantage of a weapon like thine own, and I will fight thee honestly and without flinching.'

'Nay, Sir Knight of the Round Table, but this were a merry deed withal, to help thee unto that wherewith I might perchance mount some goodly bough for the crows to peck at,' replied Tarquin.

Terrible and unceasing was the struggle, but in vain the giant knight attempted to regain the use of his sword. Then Sir Lancelot, with a wary eye, finding no hope of his life, save in the use or accomplishment of some notable stratagem, bethought him of the attempt to throw his adversary by a sudden feint. To this end he pressed against him heavily and with his whole might, then darting suddenly aside, Sir Tarquin fell to the ground with a loud cry. Sir Lancelot leapt joyfully upon him, thinking to overcome his enemy, but the latter, too cunning to be thus caught at unawares, kept his sword firmly holden, and his enemy was still unprovided with the means of defence.

Now did Sir Lancelot begin to doubt what course he should pursue, when suddenly the damsel, who, having bound up the wounds of the captive knight as he lay, and now sat a little way off watching the event, cried out, 'Sir Knight, the tree, a goodly bough for the gathering.'

Then did Sir Lancelot remember the weapons that were there, along with the shields and the body armour of the knights Sir Tarquin had vanquished. Starting up, ere his enemy had recovered himself, he snatched a broad falchion from the bough, and again defied him to the combat. But the fight was fiercer than before, so that being sore wounded, and the day exceeding hot, they were after a season fain to pause for breath.

'Thou art the bravest knight I ever encountered,' said Sir Tarquin, 'I would crave thy country and thy name, for, by my troth and the honour of my gods, I will give thee thy request on one condition, and release thy brethren of the Round Table. For why should two knights of such pith and prowess slay each other in one day?'

'And what is thy condition?' inquired Sir Lancelot.

'There liveth but one, either in Christendom or Heathenesse, unto whom I may not grant this parley, for him have I sworn to kill,' said Sir Tarquin.

"'Tis well,' replied the other, 'but what name or cognisance hath he?'

'His name is Lancelot du Lac!'

'Behold him!' was the reply, Sir Lancelot at the same time brandishing his weapon with a shout of defiance.

When Sir Tarquin heard this he gnashed his teeth for very rage.

'Now one of us must die,' said he, 'thou slewest my brother Sir Carados at Shrewsbury, and I have sworn to avenge his defeat. Thou diest. Not all the gods of thy fathers shall deliver thee.'

So to battle they went with more heat and fury than ever, and a marvel was it to behold, for each blow did seem as it would have cleft the other in twain, so deadly was the strife and hatred between them.

Sir Lancelot pressed hard upon his foe, though himself grievously wounded, and in all likelihood would have won the fight, but, as ill-luck would have it, when dealing a blow mighty enough to fell the stoutest oak in Christendom, he missed his aim, and with that stumbled to the ground. Then did Sir Tarquin shout for joy, and would have made an end of him, but that Sir Lancelot, as he lay, aimed a deadly thrust below his enemy's shield where he was left unguarded, and quickly turned his joy into tribulation, for Sir Tarquin, though not mortally wounded, drew back and cried out lustily for pain. Sir Lancelot leapt again to his feet, eager and impatient for the strife.

The contest was again doubtful, neither of them showing any disposition to yield or in any wise to abate the rigour of the conflict. Night, too, was coming on apace, and seemed like enough to pitch her tent over them, ere the issue was decided. But an event now fell out which, unexpectedly enough, terminated this adventure. From some cause arising out of the haste

and rapidity of the strokes, one of these so chanced that both had their swords suddenly driven from out of their right hands. Stooping together to retrieve their swords, by some error or enchantment, they exchanged weapons.

Then did Sir Lancelot soon find his strength to increase, whilst his adversary's vigour began to abate, and in the end Sir Lancelot slew him, and with his own sword cut off his head. He then perceived that the giant's great strength was by virtue of his sword, and that it was through his wicked sorcery therewith he had been able to overcome, and had wrought such disgrace on the Knights of the Round Table.

Sir Lancelot forthwith took the keys from the giant's girdle and proceeded to the release of the captive knights, first unbinding the prisoner who yet lay in a piteous swoon hard by. But there was a great outcry and lamentation when he saw 'twas his own brother Sir Erclos in this doleful case, for it was he whom the cruel Tarquin was leading captive when he met the just reward of his misdeeds.

After administering to his relief, Sir Lancelot rode up to the castle gate but found no entrance thereby. The drawbridge was raised, and he sought in vain the means of giving the appointed signal for its descent.

But the damsel showed him a secret place where hung a little horn. On this he blew a sharp and ringing blast, when the bridge presently began to lower, and instantly to adjust itself across the moat. Whereon, hastening, he unlocked the gate. But here he had nigh fallen into a subtle snare, by reason of an ugly dwarf that was concealed in a side niche of the wall. He was armed with a ponderous mace, and had not the maiden drawn Sir Lancelot aside by main force, he would have been crushed in its descent, the dwarf aiming a deadly blow at him as he passed. It fell, instead, with a loud crash on the pavement, and broke into a thousand fragments. Thereupon, Sir Lancelot smote him with the giant's sword, and hewed the mischievous monster asunder without mercy.

Turning towards the damsel, he beheld her form suddenly change, and she vanished from his sight. Then was he aware that it had been the nymph Viviane who accompanied him through the enchantments he had so happily subdued. He soon released his brethren, and great was the joy at the Round Table when the Knights returned to the banquet.

Thus endeth the chronicle of Sir Lancelot and Sir Tarquin, still a notable tradition in Lancelot's shire, the remains of Tarquin's castle being shown to this very day.

FRED: Leaving Martin Mere behind, with regret, we take horse to Parbold, near Ormskirk, and register at an eighteenth-century inn with a curious name, The Eagle and Child. The inn sign shows an eagle with spread wings perched above a baby in a cradle. After a couple of jars of Southport Brewery Golden Sands best bitter and a fine meal of local produce, Lily tells us the story of The Eagle and Child.

4

THE EAGLE
AND CHILD

A Gift of Eagles

Lathom House was a castellated mansion of great magnificence,
surrounded by moat and curtain wall. Sir Thomas de Lathom
was in sombre mood, morose and melancholy, unmindful of the
splendour and ostentatious wealth surrounding him. It was twelve
years to the day since he had married Ciceley Massey, youngest
daughter of Sir Hamon Massey de Dunham Massey, yet she had
failed to provide him an heir to carry on his name, merely a ten-
year-old daughter, Isabel.

Isabel was a lonely child. Her father paid her scant regard.
Her mother held her dear, but was preoccupied in trying to
appease Sir Thomas for the disappointment she had inflicted upon
him in failing to give him a son.

Sir Thomas' brooding brought forth a plan: he would adopt a
baby son, and if it were of his own flesh that would be all to the
good. He had caught the eye of a comely maid and dazzled her
with his magnificence. Mary Oskatel was her name, the daughter
of a yeoman of some substance. The plan was born.

When the child was born, Sir Thomas graciously deigned to adopt it as his own, for a fee agreed with the good yeoman. Nobody thereabouts chose to wonder too much whom the father might be, for Mary was not unknown to the local gallants, and to allay suspicion further he would call the boy Oskatel.

Sir Thomas kept in mind – however appeasing and complaisant his wife might be – Lady Ciceley would baulk at her own child being pre-empted not only by a bastard son but also one of lower rank. There was need for subterfuge.

It was the practice of Sir Thomas and Lady Ciceley to rise with the sun and to take a stroll around their extensive grounds, to enjoy the morning sights and sounds of its creatures. On this particular morning, Sir Thomas was, for once, in good spirits,

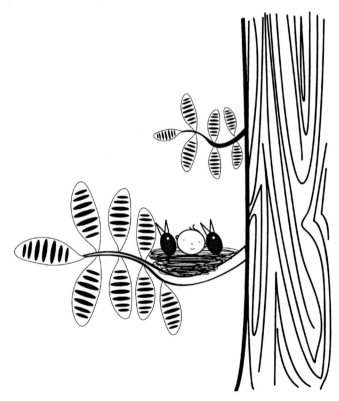

and Lady Ciceley was happy and quick to catch his mood, chattering with some hilarity at the antics of the dairy maids, whilst he guided her deftly towards an ancient and gigantic oak tree.

There had been an eagle's eyrie in this old oak since his grandfather's time. Enlarged each breeding season, it was now five feet across and three feet deep.

As they neared the oak tree, Sir Thomas paused, cocking his ear, saying in a surprised voice, 'Canst thou hear aught? It soundeth like a baby's feeble cry, and it cometh from the branches of yon tree.' He promptly began to climb the tree, as he had done many times as a boy to risk stealing eagle's eggs. He saw the present pair of eagles perched with wings spread upon the eyrie's edge, peering into the nest with, for eagles, puzzled looks. Shooing them away, he gently lifted the swaddled child from the nest, carefully climbed one-handed down the tree, and placed the baby in Lady Ciceley's arms.

She gazed at the child in her arms for some time then turned her eyes on her husband, with a look both shrewd and subtle. She saw through the subterfuge, as he knew she would. She knew he would have his way and adopt the child, whatever she might say. At the same time, she knew he had offered her a convenient fiction, a way out. He smiled at her and waited.

'Why,' she said, "tis a gift of providence which the wise eagles have brought us. We shall make him our own, and we shall call him,' she returned her husband's smile, 'Oskatel.'

THE RISE AND FALL OF OSKATEL DE LATHOM

Baby Oskatel was a delight to little Isabel. A strong bond was formed between them from the day her father and mother brought him home, and as they grew they remained inseparable companions.

Sir Thomas' intention was to share his wealth equally between his children. Lady Ciceley did not demur, for she had grown to love her adopted son. So, the boy enjoyed the dignity and privilege of noble birth, save that he could not inherit his father's title.

Oskatel was now a well-appointed young man, eager to seek a place in the court of King Edward. Isabel had blossomed into the bountiful spring of her beauty. Many young men of noble birth and rich endowment had paid court to her, men whom her father found fit for a daughter of such gentle blood and princely inheritance. Yet, none had as yet touched her heart.

It happened that Oskatel and Isabel were present at a tourney to be attended by the king. As they rode towards the pavilions, many a stately knight turned his head towards fair Lady Isabel. Her face was as lovely as the blush of rose blossom, her bosom plump and round as ripe apples in her tight décolleté bodice.

With a fanfare of trumpets, first to enter the lists was Sir John Stanley on a grey charger. A diligent student and practitioner in the art of war, Sir John had travelled and fought throughout the courts and fields of Europe to learn his trade. He wore a full suit of Italian armour with a cuirass of well-tempered steel capable of resisting a lance-stroke without being pierced or bent.

Sir John dipped his lance to the king's pavilion then turned to pay homage at the pavilion for fair dames, where his eye fell upon Isabel, and he was pierced right through his cuirass to his heart. Under his intense gaze, a bright blush bloomed in her breast and neck. In her agitation she let go her kerchief which was whisked away in the wind onto the lists, where the gallant Sir John retrieved it, and with a bow to Isabel and an impudent flourish he tied it to his lance as a token of her favour.

Another fanfare of trumpets announced the approach of the young French Admiral of Hainault on a black warhorse. His armour was beautifully wrought in blue and white and inlaid with silver, and he bore a plume of white feathers upon his helm.

The trumpets sounded. The signal was given. The lances clicked into their rests. The warhorses thundered forward. There was a mighty clash like a bolt of lightning and a cloud of dust obscured the lists. As the dust dispersed, the warriors were seen to have regained their upright stance. No injury had been sustained save the shivering of their lances. There was loud applause.

Esquires provided fresh weapons to the combatants. The Admiral, white feathers askew, trembling with vexation and rage at failing to unseat Sir John at the first foray, could barely hold back for the signal. Sir John sat back on his well-padded war saddle. On the signal, the Admiral heatedly spurred his warhorse to a gallop, its hooves pounding and churning the earth, the Admiral aiming his lance for a direct thrust at Sir John's heart.

Sir John held his warhorse back from a full gallop, placing total confidence in his steed, the support of his saddle, the strength of his armour and of his own power, and focused his entire attention on the tip of his spear. The Admiral's lance glanced off Stanley's cuirass but with the momentum of his charge he impaled himself upon Stanley's spear, its point piercing his beautifully wrought armour and mail coat.

Horse and rider rolled backwards together onto the ground, screaming piteously, covered in dust and gore. The warhorse's back was broke and it was swiftly dispatched by esquires. Grievously wounded and crushed beneath his horse, the Admiral quickly bled out and expired.

Dismounting and raising his visor, Sir John approached the gate of Isabel's pavilion, where he made a low obeisance and presented to her the stolen favour, now nobly won. Her whole frame atremble, and to tumultuous applause, she bound the favour around his arm. With the crowd shouting, 'Thy garland, lady!' Isabel carefully unwound the golden garland from around her hair, and as Sir John bowed low before her she placed it over the knight's helm.

In the presence of Sir John, delicious sensations she had never known coursed through Isabel's body, a weakening of her legs, a shivering up and down her spine, a stiffening of her breasts, a tingling in her loins. I shall have to ask the dairy maids, she thought, what these feelings might mean.

The king observed the pair with a shrewdly lascivious gleam in his eye. He called the victor and the lady whose favour he bore to his pavilion, and said, 'Sir John, I commend thee to thy mistress. She is truly the Queen of Beauty. I command thy presence and that of thy lady at my banquet.'

Waving Oskatel to her side, she said, 'My gracious liege, here is my brother. It is meet I entrust myself into his care.'

His hungry old eyes filled and thrilled by the sight of the Queen of Beauty, the king proclaimed, 'Thy brother's quality is not unknown to us. I shall honour thee, lady, by ennobling him.' Then, bidding her brother kneel, the king pronounced the words which filled the boy's heart with gladness, 'Arise, Sir Oskatel de Lathom, and with the honour of knighthood I confer upon thee the manors of Irlam and Urmston.' This was the high point in Oskatel's life.

Being of a subordinate line of the Stanley family, Sir John did not at first commend himself to Sir Thomas as an acceptable suitor for a daughter so highly born. But in view of Sir John's irresistible rise in the king's service, and his accrual of great wealth, he at last relented, and Sir John and Lady Isabel were wed.

Sir John was not a man to accept half a fortune when he could seize the whole. Knowing Sir Thomas to be a man of resolute will, determined always to pursue his chosen course, Sir John laboured with equal resolution and greater subtlety in the cause of his wife's true heritage and against the interests of the bastard Oskatel. Only on his death bed, with his daughter and son-in-law by his side, his son absent on an errand for Sir John, did Sir Thomas' conscience strike him, and he bequeathed the bulk of his fortune to Lady Isabel.

Oskatel thus lost the greater part of his inheritance, leaving him only those manors of Irlam and Urmston, conferred upon him by the king.

But for Sir John Stanley, the acquisition of Lady Isabel and of her heritage marked the beginning of a powerful Stanley dynasty, with Lathom Hall their historic family seat. The Stanleys even appropriated the image of the eagle and child, incorporating into their coat-of-arms a representation of a swaddled baby, an eagle with spread wings perched above.

LILY: There's time for another tale, with another round of Golden Sands, before we turn in. Fred particularly likes tales of powerful and resourceful women, so he is going to tell the tale of the Devil's Wall in Aughton, Ormskirk.

5

THE DEVIL'S
WALL

In an Age of Enlightenment, Gideon Chiselwig was an unenlightened and unhappy man. His mind was perpetually preoccupied – even sustained – by that malevolent bitterness and spite of which his wife Nelly bore the brunt. Gideon had built a wall between himself and Nelly, letting nothing of himself out, save the grenades of rancour and disdain which frequently he flung over the wall. Of her continuing loyalty, care and devotion, he let in nothing.

Not that Nelly was a wilting willowherb. She stood up for herself, telling him plainly, arms akimbo, when his behaviour was intolerable. Whenever he acted surly and shiftless, she nagged him and goaded him into industry. When once he made to strike her, she hefted the fire iron in her hands to fend him off.

Long ago, Nelly had been a shop girl in a small bakery in Ormskirk. With her baker's cap at a jaunty angle, a crisp white apron adorning her fulsome figure, and her floury cheeks hot from the ovens, she looked as delectable as the gingerbread that was the speciality of the shop.

One day a tall and striking young tailor entered the shop in a smart frock coat of English Broadcloth, which had been his apprentice piece. Nelly's eyes widened with admiration at the sight of Gideon, whilst Gideon's eyes feasted upon the sight of Nelly's bonny, flour-flecked comeliness.

The young lovers wandered and played together on Gaw Hill and Aughton Moss, and married at St Michael's church, Aughton. In their cottage in the village they set up a little tailoring workshop, where Nelly began to learn some simple tailoring to support her husband. The first garment she made was for Gideon. It was a heavy-grade canvas work apron with two sets of apron strings to give a close fit.

They lived happily and industriously together until, little by little, ill feeling invaded Gideon's heart and shrivelled his soul. Gideon had been a fine tailor. Now he lost patience with his profession, which demanded a diligence and stamina which his ever more morose nature could no longer endure. Oh, Gideon was brilliant at helping a customer choose his woollen or worsted fabric, taking his measurements, gauging his body's deformities and his imperfect stance, then preparing a pattern and with swift precision cutting the cloth for a suit which would smooth out such deficiencies, and finally charming the customer and smoothing his anxieties through the fittings. All else he neglected.

To make up for her husband's disregard for his work, Nelly conscientiously learnt the art and graft of tailoring. She carefully washed and drip-dried felt and canvass to shrink them for padding. She fondly stitched pockets where Gideon had chalk-marked. She caressingly padded the body of the garment, its shoulders, sleeves, collar, and pockets. She tenderly tacked the coat together and pinned on the sleeves for a first fitting. She lovingly re-cut the sleeves to the correct length and width and teased in wadding around the sleeve head before the final fitting.

Then, she painstakingly took upon herself the skilful task of finishing: sewing in the linings, stitching button holes, sewing on buttons, and stitching together the whole coat with neat, fine stitches of silk thread. Finally, she ironed her love for Gideon into the finished garment.

To Gideon's mind, Nelly bullied him, berated him, usurped his role as master tailor and master in his own home, even threatened him with the fire iron. As he became ever more envious of his wife and resentful of her actions and her manner towards him, his soul gradually sank into a pit of burning coals and clinker, as if all the demons of hell were roasting his entrails. As feelings of despair and self-loathing – from which he had hidden all his life – took hold of him, he felt the wall between himself and Nelly crumbling, for she could not fail to notice his growing misery and hopelessness.

On the tailors' grapevine, Gideon had heard the tale of a tailor in Clitheroe who, by reciting the Paternoster backwards three times, had summoned the devil and had then outwitted him. So, he resolved on a desperate enterprise, to petition the devil to reform his wife, and from the smouldering pit of his desperation and despondency there erupted a throaty roar of rough and raucous sniggering and snarling.

That very night, he wrapped a heavy cloak around his work clothes and by midnight stood in a field to the north of Gaw Hill, reciting the Paternoster backwards three times. Straightaway there came a screeching and howling in his ears as ten thousand times ten thousand fierce, fiery demons whirled around him, tearing at his flesh in their flight.

A figure rose before him, wreathed in smoke and flame, red in its light, with horns upon its head, hooves for feet, its giant bat wings raised, its face grotesque, with eyes of fire and fangs of iron, bearing a barbed spear. Gideon's flesh was scorched in the creature's searing heat. He flung off his heavy cloak and canvas apron. His bowels loosed as he faced the fearsome fiend, falling to his knees in trembling awe.

The apparition spoke, 'Thou hast summoned the Mighty One and put thyself in my power. Thou canst name two conditions to our contract, which, once fulfilled, thy soul shall be wholly mine, and thou shalt suffer the trials thou knowest all too well until the end of time. Name thy conditions.'

'Thou shalt thoroughly reform my wife,' croaked Gideon, 'that she honoureth me, offereth me nought but devotion and service, showeth me always kindness in speech and action.'

'Thy first condition is fulfilled,' the apparition at once responded, 'name thy second condition.'

Gideon thought of the agony of despair and loathing he suffered and of the crumbling wall between himself and Nelly, then uttered his second condition, 'An hour before dawn tomorrow, thou shalt build me a wall with stone and mortar, collecting all the materials thyself. It must be four hundred yards in length, an unscalable seven feet in height, and all finished by cock crow.'

'Thy second condition shall readily be fulfilled, before I enjoy thine agony for all eternity,' quoth the apparition in sonorous tones. He unfurled a great scroll, pierced Gideon's finger with his spear, and demanded he sign in blood forthwith, or else the pact would be unconditional and his soul would go straight to the pit.

Scratched, scorched, soiled and despairing of his soul, Gideon staggered home before dawn to a wife distraught by his absence. With the wall breached, Gideon tearfully poured out his story to his wife, his deepening desolation, his resentment and envy towards her, his pact with the devil, and his two conditions. Nelly listened to her husband with a concerned and discerning thoughtfulness and with her customary care and devotion. As the Mighty One had inferred, the first condition was fulfilled long before it was asked.

During the day, Nelly made her husband gingerbread and comforted him, yet without trying to reassure him that his position was not as grave as it clearly was. Then, the couple calmly discussed how Gideon might confound the devil and escape eternal torment.

An hour before dawn, Gideon had returned to the field north of Gaw Hill. A violent fit of shuddering seized his limbs, for he dreaded the devil's return, until he saw, strolling across the field towards him, a small man in the garb of a master mason. Over his shoulder he carried a heavy bag of masonry tools, picks, hammers, chisels, trowels, shovels, which on arrival he dropped to the ground. For a moment, the mason's eyes burned bright and Gideon felt their heat prickling his skin.

'Hast though all that thou needeth?' asked Gideon, 'For thou hast much to accomplish e'er the cock shall crow.'

'It shall be achieved,' replied the mason, confidently affording Gideon a devilish grin. Straightaway, he began delving in the ground with the energy – it seemed to Gideon – of a hundred miners, chucking up chunks of stone from the alluvial deposits below the topsoil. In less than half the time before cock crow, a great heap of stone had been unearthed, enough to build a four hundred yard wall seven feet high.

'So far so good,' commented Gideon, with more assurance than he felt, 'but thou hast still to mix the mortar and build the wall.'

'Very true, very true, but if thou looketh yonder, at the edge of the field, there is a pit of slaked lime left over by the farmer,' replied the smirking mason.

'Ah,' said Gideon, who appeared somewhat dismayed, 'but thou hast still to fetch several loads of sand from the sand pit beyond the moss, and thou hast no cart to carry it in.'

A momentary anxiety scuttled across the mason's features, then he said, 'There must be some container around, so I shall take a moment to cast about for it.'

'Well, I have an idea that might be helpful,' offered Gideon, contriving an expression of innocent enthusiasm, 'here is my work apron I cast aside yesternight. It is made of heavy-grade canvas and hath twin apron strings, handy for making up a bundle for carrying sand.'

Without pausing to allow the worm of suspicion to crawl in, the mason grabbed the apron from the ground, unfurled his mighty bat wings, and in a trice was streaking across the moss towards the sand pit. He soon returned with a brimming load of sand, dumped it by the heap of stones, and darted away for a second load, then a third.

He returned from his third visit to the sand pit in a thundering rage. 'Rogue! Villain! Thou dareth try to cheat the Mighty One,' he bellowed. 'The strings of thine apron snapped, dumping my last load upon the moss, but by Antichrist I shall yet make enough mortar to finish the job, then I shall compound thine eternal torment a hundredfold.'

Earlier, a shamefaced Nelly had gladly admitted to Gideon that when she had stitched on the apron strings, it had been poorly done.

The mason furled his bat wings, mixed the slaked lime with the two loads of sand into mortar, and began building the wall like a bat out of hell – as we say in Lancashire. There remained but two great stones left to lay when the mortar ran out. With no time to fetch more sand, the cock crowed over the devil's debacle. With a mortified scream he stamped the ground with his great cloven hooves, shaking the wall to its foundations, bringing the stones crashing down. A cry, heart-rending as the loss of paradise, rent the sky. The cock had summoned the devil back into the pit.

With the fiend confounded and the wall broken, Gideon could let Nelly help and guide him gradually to restore his soul, bringing happiness in place of despair, loving in place of loathing, light in place of darkness. Whenever Gideon felt threatened by demons, a walk with Nelly to the Devil's Wall brought him peace of mind. And with two talented tailors in their little workshop, their profession thrived.

FRED: We enjoy a quick breakfast of porridge, toast and tea, and leaving the publican to lodge our horses at a nearby livery stables we take a train from Ormskirk for the thirty-minute journey through the northern suburbs of Liverpool to Central Station.

We walk down to Pierhead and into the breathtaking, vast octagonal lobby of the Port of Liverpool Building. It is like a cruciform renaissance temple, and indeed it started out as one of the designs submitted for Liverpool's Anglican Cathedral. This is an awesome space for Lily to tell some Liverpool legends.

LILY: There are enough stories in Liverpool, indeed in the whole of Merseyside, to merit another book of folk tales!

6

LIVERPOOL
LEGENDS

LILY: Liverpool, although younger than Manchester, is a hotch-potch of culture, personality, clashes of history all mixed together like that traditional dish – Scouse. From tales of Irish immigrants to secret villages under the sea and other urban legends, here are a few tales to whet one's appetite for this magnificent city.

THE LIVER BIRDS

The Liver Birds are the symbol of Liverpool. Instead of being a mythical creature, they are two sea birds – cormorants – that adorn the tower of the Royal Liver Building. There are a few modern myths surrounding their importance to the city. One legend has it that if an honest man and a maiden fall in love in front of the Royal Liver Building, then the birds would come to life and fly off, this would mean the end of Liverpool. The second tale is that the birds are male and female; the female looks out to sea while the male looks back at the city, possibly to see if he could watch either Everton or Liverpool football clubs are playing at home!

THE LEPRECHAUNS OF LIVERPOOL

Liverpool has a large Irish diaspora, many of whom came from the Emerald Isle during the potato famine. As you may know, the leprechaun is the key figure in the fairy folk from that country. If you were to grab one of these magical creatures, the leprechaun would have to give you his hoard of gold. In the summer 1964 there was an outbreak of leprechaun sightings – thousands of children from Liverpool spotted little men the size of gnomes, running down Jubilee Drive and on the bowling green at Crosby. This carried on for ten days, reaching Kirby where more children saw the small folk in the churchyard of St Chad's. Eventually, the fey fever calmed down, with explanations that it was anything from collective childish imaginations to small circus folk.

THE RODNEY STREET GAMBLER

In a well-to-do part of the city there is a small burial ground. This is not an unfamiliar sight in a city; however, it is unusual as there is a pyramid in the centre. This is no Masonic tomb, rather it is the resting place of one William Mackenzie, a railway engineer and itinerant gambler.

MacKenzie was born in 1794 and died a very rich man in 1851, leaving an estate worth £341,841 to his younger brother.

Legend has it that William did not owe his success to a life spent improving Liverpool's railway infrastructure; rather it was due to his fruitful gambling habit. In this pursuit he was seemingly so lucky that one tale goes that he had made a Faustian pact with Satan in order to continually win at cards. This was probably due to the man being a staunch atheist; if you don't believe in a heaven then there's nothing to lose in gambling a soul. One cannot possibly lose that in which one does not believe.

The devil furnished William with a winning hand in every card game he played. Some might wonder why people kept playing against such a strong adversary. Maybe it was because some holier gambling men thought that their god may beat the evil one's doing. But the power of MacKenzie's cards was too strong.

Of course, MacKenzie was only mortal and he died like we all must do. The deal he had struck was that when his body was lain down in death, the devil would collect his due. But although he had been an atheist, MacKenzie had one final trick: in his will he demanded that he be buried upright with his favourite winning hand of cards clenched in his fingers.

Although old Nick can be tricked and is a little dim, it is said that despite William's final plan to ward off his soul being stolen and spirited down to hell, his tormented spirit still wanders the streets of Liverpool. In 1871, Doctor Lionel Harland heard the sound of footsteps approaching. Looking through the fog he saw a tall figure in a top hat and a flowing cape. The doctor recognised him at once, someone he had not seen for twenty years: the ghost of William MacKenzie! It is said that his face looked as though it had been lit up by the fires of hell, and that his eyes were soot black. This phantom is said to have literally scared Lionel to death!

Some of the ladies of the night over the last century have reported of being pursued by an unsavoury character who would try to be inappropriate with them. When they went to run away they heard footsteps pursuing them and when they turned there was no-one there. It seems that perhaps William did not manage to cheat the devil after all.

LILY: From the Port of Liverpool Building we take a short walk to the Liverpool One Bus Station in Canning Street, pausing to see the historic Canning Dock on the way. We take the next bus to Warrington, travelling through Broadgreen, Huyton, Cronton, Farnworth, Penketh, and Sankey Bridges.

Arriving in Warrington, we walk to St Elphin's church and gather in the chancel.

7

TALES OF BEWSEY HALL

FRED: My great-grandfather, Dr Samuel Hibbert, was a grand storyteller and collector of tales. We invite you to go back in time with us to listen in on his story around the Legend of Bewsey Hall, which he collected around the year 1900:

A group of us story collectors went to St Elphin's church to research the Legend of Bewsey Hall. Talking together in the chancel, close by the tomb of Sir John Boteler and his wife Margaret, we realised we had drawn a small crowd.

So I decided to recount the legend, 'The story is about greed, pride and power, but more than anything it is about loyalty and devotion. It is two folk tales in one, for there are alternative endings to the story, that of the loyal pageboy, and that of the faithful footman.' Here's what happened...

THE LEGEND OF BEWSEY HALL

It would be most unwise to cross Thomas Stanley, 1st Earl of Derby, Knight of the Garter, High Steward of the Duchy of Lancaster, King of Mann, stepfather to King Henry VII and godfather to his son Arthur, Prince of Wales.

Thomas Stanley was a ruthlessly ambitious and scheming man, who had repeatedly switched sides in the Wars of the Roses – always to his own advantage. At the Battle of Bosworth Field his brother William had retrieved the coronet of the slain Richard III, and it was Thomas who had placed it upon the head of the victorious Henry Tudor. From his home at Lathom House he held sway over the whole of Lancashire and beyond.

It would be deeply unwise to cross this man whose power was paramount, yet this was the risk Sir John Boteler of Bewsey Hall, Lord of Warrington, chose to take. Their argument was over a bridge across the Mersey.

As 15th Baron of Warrington, John Boteler held the monopoly for the River Mersey ferry, the only way to travel between Cheshire and Lancashire without a lengthy detour, which earned John Boteler many gross of groats.

King Henry decided on a royal progress north to visit his stepfather. The Earl of Derby pondered the inconvenience, time and danger of conveying the royal entourage, with its many persons of rank and a multitude of horses and pack mules, across the Mersey by ferry. He resolved to build a bridge. He already owned land on the Cheshire bank, and was able to purchase a parcel of ground to support the structure on the Lancashire bank, and the bridge was built.

John Boteler, finding his monopoly undermined, his ferry obsolete, and its income lost, exchanged furious words with Thomas Stanley. Not wishing to risk the royal progress being marred by acrimony, Thomas made a conciliatory gesture by inviting John to join the train of Lancastrian noblemen and gentlemen who were to accompany him to meet the monarch.

To this gesture, John Boteler made a contemptuous and discourteous refusal, which so affronted the pride and high dignity of Thomas Stanley – 1st Earl of Derby, Knight of the Garter, High Steward of the Duchy of Lancaster, and King of Mann – as to ensure John Boteler's death. Thomas Stanley's son, Lord George Stanley, together with Sir Piers Leigh and Mister William Savage, gained entry to Bewsey Hall in the dead of night by treachery and slew Sir John Boteler by his bed in the presence of his wife, Lady Margaret, and their infant son Tom.

George Stanley had bribed the disgruntled and avaricious porter at Bewsey Hall to set a light in a window to guide the murderers quietly across the broad moat in a coracle. As the solemn tongue of the old turret clock tolled one o'clock, the disloyal porter guided the three villains to Sir John's bedchamber. They had intended to make a swift end of him as he slept, only to find John's devoted chamberlain Master Houlcroft guarding his master's slumbers and barring the way to his bedchamber.

Master Houlcroft called to his master, 'Awake, Sir John! Awake and flee. These blood-hounds are on thy track.'

'We'll stop thy crowing, pretty bird! Nor flutter thy wings again,' Lord George retorted.

A swift and unequal swordfight ensued. The loyal and courageous chamberlain stood as boldly before his master's door as did Horatius defending the bridge. Undaunted, he received many savage wounds before George Stanley's sword severed his heart in twain. He fell dead, his body still loyally blocking the threshold.

The warning shouts of faithful Houlcroft and the clashing of swords had aroused Sir John, but ere he had leapt from his bed and grasped his sword, Lord George and his fellow murderers, fired up by the slaughter of the chamberlain, broke through the door and fell upon him with their bloody swords and he was swiftly hacked to the floor. With his sword inverted, clasping its hilt in both gauntleted hands, Lord George delivered a gory coup de grâce to Sir John's jugular.

THE LEGEND OF THE LOYAL PAGEBOY

To Lord George Stanley, avenging the affront to his father's pride and dignity meant not only despatching the father but altogether destroying the Boteler line. Amid Lady Margaret's anguished screams at seeing her husband cruelly slain, Lord George rushed with fury towards little Tom's cradle, his inverted sword held ready for a ferocious plunge into the vitals of the sleeping child. But to his chagrin and vexation, the cot was empty.

'We've killed the bird, but where's the egg?' he cried.

Whilst Master Houlcroft had been holding the villains at bay, a vigilant pageboy had bundled the sleeping infant into a wicker basket wrapped in a muslin cloth and hastened towards the main door of Bewsey Hall, where he was accosted by the treacherous porter.

'What hast thou there, my lad, and where doest think thou art going withal at this late hour?'

'Oh! They have slain Sir John,' the pageboy replied, his cunning words tumbling from his mouth, 'and cast his grisly head into this wicker basket and bade me run with all haste to Warrington Bridge and spike it there without delay.'

'Aye,' said the loathsome knave, heaving open the great door, 'there let his head be spiked till his grinning teeth be dry, and every day with jeer and taunt I'll mock it till I die.'

The pageboy made haste across Warrington Bridge, conveying the still sleeping child to the nearby Priory of the Hermit Friars of St Augustine, where Sir John Boteler had been a patron. From there, on the morrow, a distraught Lady Margaret was able to recover her infant son, who went on to continue the Boteler line.

Meanwhile, having searched in vain for young Tom, Lord George descended the stairs with his fellow rogues to ask the porter if anyone had left the Hall.

'No, sire.' the porter assured him, 'Only the pageboy thou didst send to Warrington Bridge with Sir John's head in a wicker basket. Now, where's the gold thou didst promise me?'

'Fool!' roared Lord George, 'Thou hast been tricked into treachery, for the head still attacheth to the carcase. Thou shalt be well paid indeed for thy master's blood and all thy services this night.'

As Lord George paid in red gold the promised fee, the porter laughed out loud, rubbing his hands with glee. Then they took him into Bewsey Park and hanged him from a tree.

THE LEGEND OF THE FAITHFUL FOOTMAN

There is another ending to the story, and here it is.

Hearing the shouts and clashes of affray in his master's bedroom from the nurse's adjoining chamber, a negro footman*, with great presence of mind, rushed in, snatched up the infant Tom from his cradle and carried him to his nurse. Slamming the door behind him, the footman pressed his shoulder to the door with all his strength of will and sinew. Finally, when by sheer weight against the door the three butchers broke through, the loyal footman held them off further with his flaying fists. By the time he was overcome and slain, the nurse had escaped with young Tom, who was now

---

*The authors employ the now deprecated term 'negro footman' for the sake of authenticity.

under the protection of the Hermit Friars of St Augustine, saved by the sacrifice of a faithful footman, to continue the Boteler line.

Lady Margaret raised an alabaster tomb, in the Bewsey Chapel of St Elphin's parish church in Warrington. On this tomb is depicted the figure of the self-sacrificing footman, his body buried alongside his master, and in time his mistress also, as the last earthly reward which could be paid him for preserving the life of the infant heir to the Boteler estate.

We had been so engrossed in the story, we had not noticed a young woman standing listening by the Boteler tomb. Now she came forward and spoke to us, 'Well, that sure is a fine tale, though the real story is far darker.'

The woman had soft dark curls in a Gibson Girl style. She wore a smart, white shirtwaist with a high collar and a dark green ankle-length skirt with matching jacket. Her face was more compelling than pretty, with animated features and a direct look. For a young woman of barely twenty summers, her voice was firm and assured, 'My name is Mabel Cecilia Atwood and I am from Lancaster County, Nebraska. My family emigrated to America in the seventeenth century, and I am here in England on a pilgrimage to visit my English ancestors, whose names and histories are faithfully recorded in our family bible, all the way back fourteen generations to John and Margaret Boteler, who are buried right here. Now, if you will allow, I will tell you their story.'

THE VENGEANCE OF THOMAS STANLEY

First of all, let me tell you, when John Boteler was murdered, Thomas Stanley was only twenty-eight years old, his children were mere infants, and he was not to become 1st Earl of Derby for another twenty-two years. It was his father, Thomas Stanley, Lord of Lathom, who disputed with John Boteler over the Warrington bridge and it was young Thomas Stanley himself who murdered him. Now, here's the story …

Thomas, Lord of Lathom was a diplomat. It would be typical of him, as your story suggests, to make overtures to John Boteler to settle their quarrel. His son Thomas Stanley would never stoop to diplomacy where duplicity or brute force would suffice. It was said of Thomas, Lord of Lathom, after his death, 'He was brave in the field, wise in the Senate, just to his Prince, an honour to his country, and an ornament to his family.'

An ornament he certainly was, but rarely a living presence in the family home. As a lawyer and diplomat he was more often in Ireland or Scotland or Calais or otherwise serving in the King's Household.

Thomas, Lord of Lathom, and his wife Joan had seven children, of whom Thomas, William, John and Margaret were around the same age. With Joan weakened by constant childbearing and her husband largely absent, a pecking order was early established between these four children. Thomas, slightly older, was lord, with William his lieutenant. John and Margaret were the underdogs, as we say in America.

In the absence of parental control, the behaviour of Thomas and William was unrestrained in the cruelty inflicted upon their siblings. Long before the Battles of Blore Heath and Bosworth Field were the Battles of Lathom House. Thomas and William were invariably the victors, and the vanquished were subjected to savage beatings and mock beheadings, to being chained and locked in dungeons.

The only respite for John and Margaret were the occasional visits to Bewsey Hall, the home of John Boteler, 14th Baron of Warrington. His son John, being six or seven years older than the Stanley children, had the height and strength, in their battles, to overpower Thomas and William, who suffered the indignity and hurt pride of being the vanquished, to the evident satisfaction of John and Margaret. In Thomas especially, this affront to his overweening vanity engendered an enduring, vengeful enmity towards the young John Boteler.

At the age of twenty-one, Margaret was married off to Sir William Troutbeck of Dunham, another brute man of the sword and in Thomas' eyes a worthy match for his despised sister. After fathering five children on Margaret, William Troutbeck was slain at the Battle of Blore Heath. As a widow, Margaret wasted no time in marrying her first love, John Boteler, now 15th Baron of Warrington, to the fury of her brother Thomas.

When the dispute arose about Warrington bridge between John Boteler and Thomas' father, now Baron Stanley, Thomas wanted to resolve the matter by violent means, but the baron restrained him, and continued to seek a diplomatic solution to the day of his death.

Released from his father's restraining hand, Thomas resolved to wreak long cherished vengeance upon his childhood adversary. As you have heard, Thomas Stanley slew his brother-in-law, John Boteler, and would have slain his own nephew Tom, had not the footman blocked his way and proved, in his death, to be the more valiant.

'Finishing her tale, Mabel Cecilia stepped across to the tomb where John and Margaret Boteler's effigies lay hand in hand, and placed her small hand on theirs. We stood with her in solemn silence, dwelling upon the three who shared this ancient tomb.'

FRED: We invite you to stand for a moment with Samuel Hibbert and Mabel Cecilia Atwood and share this moment so sacred to storytellers.

8

The Song of Warrikin Fair, Warrington

Fred: My great-grandfather, Dr Samuel Hibbert, continues his tale:

'After meeting Mabel Cecilia Atwood at St Elphin's and hearing her tale, Mabel and I and our group of story collectors retired to the Patten Arms Hotel.

'We were talking quietly about her visit to England and what she planned to do, when a little old man, dapper and spritely, entered the lounge and came straight over to us.

'"Good story you told, Sir," he addressed Samuel with clipped speech, "Hope you didn't mind me listening in. Verger of St Elphin's, you see."

'Then, turning to Mabel, he added, "Good to hear your piece, too, Miss. Always thought there was more to that story. Now I know. So, if you'll allow, in return I should like to tell you a story in song. Warrikin Fair. Oldest ballad in Lancashire."

'He told us that Randle Shay, who appears in the story, was Sir Thomas Boteler's bailiff in the sixteenth century.

'We said we should like to hear his song very much, at which he sat at the piano and began to sing in a rich tenor voice to a jaunty tune and, to our surprise, in a broad Lancashire dialect.

Warrikin Fair

Now, au yo' good gentlefoak, an yo' won tarry,
I'll tell yo' how Gilbert Scott soud his mare Barry;
He soud his mare Barry at Warrikin fair,
But when he'll be paid, he knaws no', I'll swear.

So when he coom whom, and toud his wife Grace,
Hoo stud up o' th' kippo, and swat him o'er th' face,
Hoo pick'd him o' th' hillock, and be fawd wi' a whack,
That he thowt would welly a broken his back.

'O woife,' quo' he, 'if thou'll le'mme but rise,
I'll gi' thee aw' th' leet, wence, imme that lies.'
'Tho udgit,' quo' hoo, 'but wheer does he dwell?'
'By lakin,' quo' he, 'that I conno tell.'

'I tuck him for t' be some gentlemon's son,
For he spent tuppence on me, when he had dun;
An' he gen me a lunchin o' denty snig poy,
An' by th' hond did he shak' me most lovingly.'

Then Grace hoo prompted her neatly and fine,
An' to Warrikin went o' We'nsday betime;
An' theer, too, hoo staid for foive markit days,
Till th' mon wi' th' mare cum to Randle Shay's.

An' as hoo wer' resting one day in hur rowm,
Hoo spoy'd th' mon a-riding th' mare into the town;
Then bounce goes hur heart, and hoo were so gloppen,
That out o' th' winder hoo'd like for to loppen.

Hoo stampt an' hoo stared, an' down stairs hoo run
Wi' hur heart in her hont, an' hur wint welly gone;
Her head-gear flew off, an' so did her snood ;
Hoo stampt an' hoo stared, as if hoo'd bin woode,

To Randle's hoo hied, an' hoo hov' up the latch,
Afore th' mon had tied th' mare gradely to th' cratch.
'My gud mon,' quo' hoo, 'Gilbert greets you right merry
And begs that yo'll send him th' money for Barry,'

'Oh, money,' quo' he, 'that connot I spare.'
'Be lakin,' quo' hoo, 'then I'll ha' the mare.'
Hoo poo'd an' hoo thrumper'd him sham' to be seen,
'Thou hangman,' quo' hoo, 'I'll poo' out thy e'en.

'I'll mak' thee a sompan, I'll houd thee a groat;
I'll auther ha' th' money, or poo' out thy throat';
So between 'em they made sich a wearisom' din,
That to mak' 'em at peace, Randle Shay did come in.

'Cum, fye, naunty Grace; cum, fye, an' ha' dun ;
You'st ha' th' mare, or th' money, whether yo' won.'
So Grace geet th' money, an' whomwards hoo's gone;
But hoo keeps it hursel' an' gies Gilbert Scott none.

'Though we hadn't understood it all, we gave our soloist an enthusiastic round of applause and invited him to partake of a whisky and soda, which he heartily accepted.'

LILY: With that we shall retire ourselves to the Patten Arms Hotel for a whisky and soda and a good night's rest.

WARRINGTON TO MANCHESTER

LILY: We leave the Patten Arms Hotel after an early breakfast, only to find ourselves transported back in time to the year 1905.

It's such a lovely day, we have arranged a Landau horse-drawn carriage with a pair of greys to take us on the next stage of our storytelling journey. We travel west with the early morning sun behind us to the magnificent, newly opened Widnes-Runcorn Transporter Bridge at the Runcorn Gap, to carry us over the Mersey and the Manchester Ship Canal.

The pair of horses step gingerly onto the car of the Transporter Bridge, whose 180ft towers support a suspended girder of 1,000ft span which carries the car beneath. Give thanks for clement weather and enjoy the splendid views as we swing twelve feet above the Mersey during our three-minute crossing.

We alight from the Landau at the Runcorn wharf of the Duke of Bridgewater's Canal and take the passenger barge on the leisurely and picturesque route to Manchester. We pause for a relaxed lunch at the Barge Inn at Monton, looking across the canal to the curious and unique lighthouse so far from the sea.

We make a detour to travel over the Barton Swing Aqueduct at Barton upon Irwell, the first and only one of its kind in the world. This remarkable construction carries the Duke of Bridgewater's Canal across the Manchester Ship Canal. The swinging action allows large vessels using the Ship Canal to pass underneath and narrowboats to cross over the top.

We arrive at the Manchester wharf ready for dinner and more tales. Fred waxes lyrical about one of his favourite cities.

9

MANCHESTER
BATTLES

In my opinion, Manchester is England's second city. Even in 1724, it was said that it was the largest, richest and busiest village in England! There has always been industry in Manchester; fabrics were dyed in the town from as early as the mid-thirteenth century. The fabric and cotton industry made Manchester rich, and the city and its nearby towns are famous for invention; many of the instruments used in the city's cotton trade were developed in the city and its nearby towns. James Kay from Bury invented the flying shuttle in 1733. James Hargreaves from Bolton made the spinning jenny in 1764, and in 1775, Sam Cromton, also from Bolton, invented the 'mule', another instrument of the weaving trade.

This hive of industry is represented by the image of a bee. The useful insect is repeated in the mosaic in the beautiful town hall. Today, you can see the image of the bee throughout the city – in honour of its past and in honour of people working together, busy as bees.

As J. Wood puts it in the book *The Story of Manchester*: 'The name Manchester to foreigners calls up an image of grey skies, murky buildings and muddy streets. Yet, in spite of the disadvantages of the city, there is a certain charm about Manchester people. In truth, this city, so modern in appearance, is a veritable home of romance.'

Manchester has always been on the cutting edge of industry, science, music and revolution. As well as romance, Manchester is no stranger to fights – witness the odd bout of fisticuffs on a Saturday night! Mancunians are a passionate lot, from the Roman warriors who settled in 'Mamucium' to the siege of Manchester, from the horror of Peterloo, to industrial revolution, socialism and the suffragettes.

Speaking of Peterloo, this was a dark moment in Manchester's history. The pub, the Briton's Protection, is not far from St Peter's Square, the scene of the massacre. It was said that here people who had been attacked by the yeomanry were ministered to. It is fitting that today many traditional tales are kept alive here with a long-running storytelling night, Word Of Mouth.

One final thing you should know about Manchester. The city is not renowned for clement weather: if you're going to visit, don't forget your brolly!

THE SIEGE OF MANCHESTER

Lancashire was divided during the English Civil War (1641–1651), with Oliver Cromwell's Parliamentarians (the Roundheads) versus the Royalists (Cavaliers). Prominent aristocrat, Lord Strange, was a leader of the Cavaliers who had seized weapons from Lancaster, Preston, Liverpool and Warrington. He had his beady eye on Manchester which had declared itself Parliamentarian.

John Rosworm was a German man who had settled in Manchester. He had fought in Europe and his military skills were well renowned. He had offered his services to both sides. However, as he lived in Manchester, it is said that he made his first offer there – finding himself on the side of the Roundheads. And so, in 1642, Rosworm served the Parliamentarian cause during the English Civil War for the sum of £30 for six months' service.

Manchester awaited Lord Strange and the army of Royalists who feared his appearance every day. With Roswell's skills in fortification, Manchester was secured. Yet the townspeople still anticipated

Strange. On 15 July 1642, Strange arrived in Manchester and a fight broke out where a linen weaver was killed – the first to die in the city's involvement in the bloody Civil War.

Strange left Manchester to regroup; the inhabitants of Manchester were expecting Strange to return at any moment.

Rosworm fought the Royalists in September 1642. The heavy rain lashed down as both sides marched along the Irwell and the Mersey towards Salford. The battle came to a head on Deansgate where the Royalists were defeated. Lord Strange was eventually executed in Bolton in 1644. Rosworm moved to London where he complained of having pledged his 'faithfulnesse to this ungratefull town'. He was sporadically paid by, as he put it, the 'promise-breakers' of Manchester. He is thought to have died during the Restoration, when King Charles II, the 'Party King' was restored to the throne.

FRED: In the morning we pack a picnic and set outside. Here we catch the bus from Shudehill to travel to Worsley, a pretty village in the borough of Salford. It's a beautiful day so we sit on a blanket near the Bridgewater Canal. There's a statue of Francis, 3rd Duke of Bridgewater in Worsley Green. He's known as 'the Canal Duke' as he founded the great canal. We open egg barmcakes from greaseproof paper, and unwrap pork pies shining with gelatine. In between bites, Lily will now tell some stories from Salford and Oldham that her auntie told her when she was little.

10

SIR ELIAS GIGAS, THE GIANT OF WORSLEY

The town of Worsley in the borough of Salford receives its name from a baronetcy. The town measures 4½ miles east to west and Worsley Hall is almost in the centre. At Daubhole in Worsley there is a great boulder known as the Giant's stone, legend has it that it was thrown from Rivington pike.

Although there is little accurate historical detail about Elias de Worsley, the founder of the town, what little is gleaned makes for wonderful tales of derring do. It also leads to the intriguing claim that Elias was a giant. And why let historical facts get in the way of a good story?!

Sir Elias – also known as Eliseus de Workesley – was one of the first Norman barons; he was born in Barton-Upon-Irwell around 1150. He was also one of the first Norman barons who raised his vassals and joined in the first crusade.

Elias was good friends with Robert Curthorse, Duke of Normandy and eldest son of William the Conqueror. Although the rules of primogeniture would have it that Robert was due the English throne upon William's death, he was an unsuccessful claimant. While his patronage and friendship to Elias was valuable, Robert was reputed to be lazy, always one for a new scam, and quarrelsome. One disagreement with his brother led to him having a chamber pot poured over his head.

He was smelling sweeter when he met Elias, although Robert was poor and up to some other scam where he was trying to wed a young bride in order to suck up her dowry.

Elias' personal acquaintance with Robert, Duke of Normandy is said to have induced him to accompany his friend and patron in attempting to rescue the Holy Land from the hands of the Saracens.

During the First Crusade, Elias met many enemies. He muscled his way through Saracens, slaughtering them with his massive, bare hands. He conquered other giants with his might. He bashed his way through dragons and conquered countless other supernatural beings.

Victorious, Elias made his way to Rhodes. Buoyed by his successful killing spree in the Levant, he encountered a vicious, venomous serpent. This beast was devastating the district, the people entreated him to sort it out as his reputation had arrived on the Grecian island several days before the man himself had.

The battle between man and cold-blooded beast was immense. The serpent coiled back in rage and sprang. Sir Elias hit it with the back of his sword. The snake-like being hissed and spat venomous poison. Elias then kicked the serpent in its painful spot - directly in the rectum.

In retaliation, the serpent bit him so severely that Elias died on the spot. Elias was then buried in Rhodes, and it is said that no native species of snake in Rhodes is venomous now, thanks to the brave giant from Lancashire.

11

THE SKULL
HOUSE

Wardley Hall in Salford is a beautiful old house built around the time of the reign of Edward VI. It is black, white and half-timbered. With its oak beams and mullion windows, it looks a lot like Middleton's Tonge Hall. However, unlike other houses from that period, for over two centuries it had something additional – the presence of a human skull kept in a special niche in the wall of a staircase. Thanks to this unusual ornament, it is known locally as Skull House. And there are two stories as to why this is; the first is a rather gory tale.

During the seventeenth century, the skull was believed to be that of Roger Downes, son of the then incumbent John Downes. Roger was a fully sworn in member of the sort of lifestyle that Charles II would have envied. He was a licentious, merry yet foolhardy man. During one of his drunken orgies, he gloated to his friends that he would 'kill the first man he met' on the way home. The unfortunate victim was a poor tailor whom Roger gleefully dispatched.

This murder brought Roger to court. However, as an aristocrat with great influence in society, he was let off, so he set back on his carousing chaotic ways. During a trip to London, in another fit of characteristic alcoholic abandon, Roger started a fight with some watchmen. This was a bit of a stupid move on the part of Roger as one of them decapitated him. It was said that his body was thrown unceremoniously into the Thames. The watchman then packed up the young lord's head into a wooden box and posted it up to Wardley Hall only to be opened by his shocked sister.

This rather amusing and gory story is just one of a few stories of how Roger met his sticky end; another tale tells that his life ended at pretty Epsom Wells where his head was parted from his body.

While this is a great story, it was rejected and disproved a century after his death when his coffin was opened in 1779. Roger's skeleton was intact, yet the upper portion of his skull had been sawn off above the eyes, presumably for some form of post-mortem investigation.

The second tale preferred by historians is that the skull belonged to a holy man. Edward 'Saint Ambrose' Barlow, Order of Saint Benedict, was the fourth son of Sir Alexander Barlow of Barlow Hall, Didsbury. He was born in Manchester, 1585. As Catholicism was frowned upon at the time, he travelled to both France and Spain where he studied to become a priest. He returned to England in 1615 to preach to those who were Roman Catholic in between Liverpool and Manchester.

He was known to travel by foot when he delivered Mass and his two main centres were the halls of Wardley and Morleys. He was set upon by Protestants, tipped off by either the vicar of Eccles or Leigh after Holy Mass on Easter Sunday, 1641. An angry mob rounded on the priest and he was arrested and taken to Lancaster Castle. He was in the meagre and miserable surroundings of Lancaster Gaol for four months before he was taken to court. Accused of being a Catholic, he was found guilty and condemned to be hanged, drawn and quartered. On 10 September 1641, this awful sentence was carried out, he was carried to his doom carrying a small wooden cross that he had made in prison.

It is said that the Ambrose's head was severed from his body and returned to Manchester as a warning to others not to practice the Catholic faith. However, Francis Downes of Wardley Hall and a secret and staunch Catholics rescued the skull and placed it in Wardley Hall.

The skull was discovered during the time of the Jacobite rebellion, when Wardley Hall was ransacked by the Young Pretender's troops. Parts of the hall were demolished in order to be made safe again and a casket was discovered containing a skull 'furnished with a goodly set of teeth and having on it a good deal of auburn hair'. As it was reputed that Ambrose had red hair, tradition has held that it is his skull that still resides today in the hall.

12

HANNAH BESWICK, THE MANCHESTER MUMMY

This rather odd story has its beginnings in 1745, when Prince Charles Edward, the Young Pretender, was marching south with his Highlanders. He pillaged and plundered, until he was turned back after being defeated at the Battle of Derby.

Meanwhile, in Hollinwood, Oldham, there was a fine mansion called Birchen Bower. It was home to Hannah Beswick, the last of the Beswick family. Hannah was renowned as an eccentric woman who kept herself to herself, yet was known affectionately to the villagers as Madam Hannah.

When the Highland hordes were sweeping south, Hannah worried for her wealth so she converted some of her possessions into gold and hid it in the grounds of the manor house. Hannah never married and farmed the land on Birchen Bower until she was too frail to do so. When she finally retired, she moved from the mansion to a cottage situated in the grounds of the manor. The Scots never came to Birchen Bower and she lived on for another thirteen years. Shortly before her death, the old lady told her relatives that if they were to carry her to the house so that she could die there, she would show them the location of the hidden gold. However, before this could be done, her condition deteriorated. She died, never revealing the location of her loot.

In the mid-eighteenth century there was an upsurge in people being afraid of being buried alive by mistake. This was due to several reported incidents during the century. Physicians began to check for signs of life from pouring pepper and vinegar into the mouths of supposed corpses, or poking sensitive areas of the body with hot metal in order to elicit a reaction. Hannah, quite understandably, did not wish to suffer the same fate. This fear was enhanced when her brother John died – or, at least, appeared to do so. He was placed in the coffin by the funeral director as Hannah wept. It was just before the lid was screwed down that Hannah noticed John's eyelids flickering. Charles White, the family practitioner, checked and showed that the man was still alive.

John was taken from out of his coffin and awoke from his coma a few days later. John lived on for many more years, after having narrowly escaped his premature burial. This event made such an impression on Hannah Beswick that she immediately made out her will, leaving her whole estate to Dr White. However, in order for White and his descendants to benefit from Birchen Bower's income, she insisted that her body should not be buried. She further stipulated that her lifeless corpse should be returned to the house every twenty-one years.

When Hannah died, Charles carried out her wishes. Charles was quite a genial looking man with wavy hair, a bulbous nose, deep-set eyes and quizzical eyebrows. He was interested in anatomy and had a collection of 'wet' and 'dry' exhibits. When he died, his macabre collection of curiosities not only included the embalmed body of Hannah Beswick, but also the body of Thomas Higgins, a notorious highwayman hanged for burglary.

The process of embalming was a precise art harking back to the mummies of ancient Egypt and having roots in the popular practice of taxidermy. It involved the veins and arteries being injected with turpentine and vermilion derived from toxic mercury. As much blood as possible needed to be squeezed out of the corpse. The organs were removed from the chest and abdomen, and then placed in water to clean them and reduce their bulk. The body was then washed with alcohol. Body cavities were filled with a mixture of camphor (for scent), nitre (for preservation and prevention of bacteria), and resin (used as a varnish or adhesive). The body was then sewn up and all openings were filled with camphor from rosemary or synthetically derived from turpentine.

After a final washing, the body could then be packed in a box containing plaster of Paris to absorb any moisture. The body was then coated in tar to preserve it.

Once mummified, Charles kept Hannah at his property in King Street Manchester, and then when he moved in Sale, Cheshire in the case of a grandfather clock.

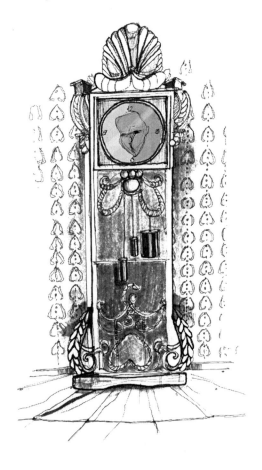

It is said that Charles lived quite comfortably off the wealth he was bequeathed by Hannah Beswick. This was carried out until 1837, her body then went on display at Manchester Museum as a modern curio until 1868 when her body was finally interred in Harpurhey Cemetery – 110 years after her death.

But the strange story does not end there. Wearing a black gown and white lace cap, the ghost of Madam Hannah was said to haunt the area where Birchen Bower had been, restless that her wishes had not been fulfilled. There were reports of poltergeist activity around the area, including a tale of a cow being transported into a hayloft by unknown means. Reports of her spectre became more and more frightening as time went by.

Eventually, the area that was Birchen Bower was transformed by industry and people forgot about the ghost of Hannah. That was until the 1950s and 1970s, when it was said that a 'grey lady' had been spotted by a couple of lads working at the old Ferranti factory. If you squint your eyes in the half-light of an evening, sometimes you can see the ghostly old lady wandering along the pavement.

LILY: Fred looked a little green around the gills when I recounted how a body was embalmed! We pack up our picnic and hop on a bus to Walkden. Nipping onto the train we take the short journey to the magnificent Victoria Station in Manchester. A quick cup of coffee then onto the train to Mills Hill. We take the short walk into Middleton and set up at the legendary Boar's Head pub where the landlord has kindly offered to put us up for the night. Fred likes a nice pint, so he'll tell you some stories about Middleton and Rochdale. Including the time he huffed and puffed as he climbed up to the summit of Blackstone Edge.

13

TALES FROM MIDDLETON

TWO LORD ASSHETONS

Generations of Assheton were Lords of the Manor of Middleton, from the 1360s until around 1765. Here are two very different men from the family, Ralph and his grandson Richard.

The first Assheton to lord it over Middleton was Ralph. Lord Ralph was reputed to have had an evil streak. In Easter time, as an old pagan ritual, the poor of the village planted spring flowers – corn marigolds – to chase the winter out and welcome in spring. As a religious man, Lord Ralph was having none of this, he rode down to Ashton-Under-Lyne in Tameside and executed anyone who had planted the golden flowers. Because of this he became known as the 'Black Knight'. Nowadays, on Easter Monday locals from Ashton have revived a tradition of parading an effigy of him cast as Black Knight around the town. They then burn this straw effigy to commemorate him and the murdered peasants of Ashton.

SECRET TUNNELS UNDER MIDDLETON

Legend has it that there was a tunnel connecting both the Ring O' Bells and The Old Boars Head pubs to Middleton parish church. The cellars of the Ring O'Bells, one of Middleton's oldest buildings, is said to be haunted by Edward the Sad Cavalier.

The local tale tells that Edward was the son of Lord Stannycliffe. During the English Civil War, the family were Royalists. Unfortunately for these loyal monarchists at the time of Cromwell's rule, Middleton was Parliamentarian and swarming with his Model Army. The Old Boar's Head was said to be the headquarters of Cromwell's Roundheads – out of bounds for Edward and his motley crew of Cavaliers.

In order to keep their loyalty a secret, Edward and a small band of men met in the Ring O'Bells cellars in order to plot the downfall of the Roundheads. They met so that if they were disturbed, they could escape to the parish church and seek refuge. Sadly, for poor Edward, one night he was betrayed. The Roundheads came to kill the young Stannycliffe, so he fled through the pub into the cellars. He ran down the passageway in order to evade the oncoming army, but he was caught in the dark and hacked to pieces by the Roundheads.

His remains were never found, and to this day he is still said to haunt the Ring O'Bells. Some nights the forlorn phantom knocks glasses over, and once threw stones. If you're in there for a pint one night, there is a chair in the snug which is never warm. It's almost as if Edward is there, still sullen by his thwarted mission, maybe you could buy him a round to cheer him up.

SIR RICHARD ASSHETON AND MIDDLETON PARISH CHURCH'S FLODDEN WINDOW

In Middleton's parish church – supposed nexus of the tunnels from the Boar's Head and Ring O'Bells – there are many stories in the stonework. The site of the church itself dates back to AD 880 and became St Leonard's in 1066. It was altered and rebuilt over the next few hundred years and is one of a few churches with a mediaeval-style wooden steeple. The church benefited from the Lord of the Manor, Richard Assheton. Unlike his grandfather Ralph, Assheton proved himself to be a true local hero in battle. In 1513, Assheton lead a successful campaign against King James IV and his army – the Battle of Flodden. He recruited archers from the town who sported longbows made from yew – flexible and strong in the heart of the wood – and metal-tipped arrows. Assheton, and the famous archers, marched from Middleton to Branxton in Northumbria to join other forces from around the country. This was a success: with many Scots and James killed the English armies drove the Scottish back over the border.

Because of his success, Assheton was knighted; he commissioned a colourful stained-glass window depicting the battle of Flodden field which was installed in his honour. He also bequeathed his standard and armour to the church, including a ceremonial boars head funeral helmet. The boar is a symbol of the family.

DICK TURPIN STOPS FOR A PINT IN MIDDLETON

The infamous Dick Turpin was executed at the young age of thirty-three. Turpin was born in Essex and is purported to have ridden from London to York holding up carriages and robbing the rich incumbents. There have been many a bawdy ballad written and sung about his adventures. Fact has turned into romanticised fiction as the highwayman was reputed to have popped in for a pint in a Middleton pub en route to his next bout of 'stand and deliver'.

The remains of the pub, which became the Grapes Inn, now lie underneath Clarke Brow playing field, the jury is still out as to whether any of the highwayman's effects – a tankard, or maybe some loot – are buried under there too.

14

TALES FROM
THE BOROUGH
OF ROCHDALE

LILY: Fred has an old book about Manchester. Here's a quote from 1795 that is quite cheeky about the borough: 'Rochdale and its vicinity may be considered as the centre of the genuine Lancashire dialect, a variety of the English tongue, which, though uncouth to the ear, and widely differs in words and grammar from cultivated language is yet possessed of much force and expression.'

If Rochdale is the epicentre of the Lancashire dialect, then it's also home to many wonderful stories and the Co-operative Movement. There are modern day reportings of unidentified flying objects, supernatural natural stories, and hauntings in some of the borough's oldest buildings. Here are some of the most popular legends of Rochdale and its surrounding areas.

DEMONS IN THE BRICKWORK

Saint Chad's church stands proud above a water spring and the grand Town Hall; its surrounding Saxon walls are perfectly placed together, carved with daisies. It is a grand building with grotesques studding the wall and fine stained glass.

There has always been a church in this spot; however, when the church was first being built, the top of the hill was not the first spot intended for it. The original site was by the shore of the Roche, the river which gives the town its name.

Many years ago, Gamel, the then Lord of the town, wanted to build a chapel close to the bank of the Roche. Gamel was a pious man who had no truck with pagans. He believed that a grand building by the waterside would be appropriate to please God.

He employed the strongest men in Rochdale, who worked from morning until sundown laying the holy building's foundations. The first day was a rare hot day; the men toiled and sweated, united in their task. That evening, to soothe their aching bones, many slept, some partook of a pint or two of fine ale in the local tavern. (For we all know that the finest ale in the land is found in Lancashire.)

In the morning, the men woke to continue their duty to Gamel. However, when they reached the riverbank they found that the stones, and all the posts they had carefully lain the previous day, had disappeared without a trace.

Fearful of Gamel, the men began again in haste. They slammed down posts; they pushed the stones deep into the land. They were firm this time. When sundown came, they were too tired to enjoy any carousing.

Early the next morning, the men returned to the north bank of the river. Again, the stones had miraculously vanished; no evidence of a bit of rubble or wood was to be seen. The builders took it as an evil omen and went to Gamel. They feared that goblins or pagan spirits, angered by a new Christian god, were seeking their revenge and had spirited the chapel away.

Gamel was angry at first, and suspected mortal trickery was to blame. He demanded that the men build again and that he would inspect it the next day. Once again, the men undertook back-breaking work.

The next day, Gamel went to see for himself that his desired building was nowhere to be seen. Fearing a malevolent presence, he then demanded that the chapel be relocated to the top of the hill overlooking the town. The place of worship was again built during the day and this time the rocks did not move. Gamel ordered that one hundred and twenty-two steps be cut into the hillside so the townspeople could traverse up to worship there.

Today, St Chad's Chapel still stands at the top of the hill. Was it demons, pagan spirits or just pranksters who thwarted the building of a waterside chapel? Maybe if you look into the waters of Packer Spout, which fed Rochdale's first reservoir, you may see a cheeky supernatural face. Whoever knows, if you count the Packer Steps up to the church, you'll find that there are one hundred and twenty-two.

THE BAUM RABBIT

Possibly the least scary of all ghost stories is the tale of the Baum rabbit. This phantom bunny would haunt the churchyard of St Mary in the Baum, instilling a mild fear in any who met the lapid in the moonlight. Moonbeams would catch the fur of the lively creature, which was said to be plump and whiter than snow.

It munched happily on herbs – lemon balm and white mint – that grew in the graveyard.

However, there is another story attached to the bunny. When the Black Death swooped over England, the Earl of Oxford was travelling over Blackstone Edge. His heart was loveworn as he could not have the woman he wanted: the beautiful Blanche. As the Earl traversed over the rocky moorland and dramatic precipice of the Edge, he wished with all his heart that his true love would be spared from the plague.

It seems that fairies heard his wishes; a pack of cards appeared with new suits of rabbits, roses, pinks and celandine. He chose the rabbit card and a pure white rabbit, wearing a golden band around its neck, appeared. The Earl sped to Rochdale to give this preternatural gift to his love, who was suffering in the final throes of illness. Without delay, the Earl gave her the rabbit and she miraculously regained her strength and recovered from a deadly malady that had already claimed so many lives. It was a cruel irony that the luckless Earl was then struck with plague and died.

The rabbit is reputed to have stayed around the area protecting the people of Rochdale. Once the plague was over,

the rabbit vanished as mysteriously as it had arrived. It was then that it began its nightly haunt around the graves of St Mary in the Baum.

RUSHBEARING FESTIVAL

In the tenth century, Pope Gregory decreed that rushes should be lain in churches on its saints day to celebrate the gain of churches from pagans, and to keep the floor, often made of stone and earth, warm. In Lancashire and Yorkshire, there became a tradition for young townsmen to gather the rushes and lay them on the floor of the church.

As the years went on, this folk practice became a festival. In Rochdale it was normally celebrated in August. It was like a carnival: there were gaily coloured carts with rushes tied in bundles and piled in stiff green pyramids on them, the buildings lining Yorkshire street and along St Mary's Gate were decorated. The carts met at noon to traverse the streets of Rochdale.

There were banners declaring dedications to God. There were street stalls selling sweet treats like Eccles cake and gingerbread. There was a cacophony of sound from bands, the growls of baited bears, crowds singing, young girls in white and green twirling, morris men clacking their sticks and dancing along. The spectacle became more dazzling with each year, so much so that in Victorian times – where the mood of the nation had become more austere – rushbearing was banned for encouraging drunkenness and lewd behaviour.

The practice of rushbearing was not driven out from the country; it's a tradition still practised in Grasmere. As for Rochdale, in 1991 Morris dancers from nearby Marsden and Littleborough revived the ancient tradition and celebrate rushbearing today.

Robin Hood and the Fairies on Blackstone Edge

Blackstone Edge is a brooding grit-stone precipice; the natural border between Lancashire and Yorkshire. There is a portion of the old Roman Road that struck out from Manchester to Yorkshire leading up to the ridge. On a clear day, there are sights of the Derbyshire peaks, Bolton's Winter Hill, and the heart-shaped Hollingworth Lake.

There are many legends attached to the Edge. A few of these involve the hero Robin Hood. At the highest point of the Edge is a rock formation, with 'Robin Hood's Bed' one of its features. One story tells that one of the boulders from the Edge was thrown eight miles by the feature was actually created by Robin Hood throwing the rock.

While the folk tale is a little murky, one of the most popular stories goes that one rain-sodden day, Robin and his men were travelling over the West Riding of Yorkshire towards Rochdale. The weak bleats of sheep punctuated their journey. Wind whipped and wet through, Robin was exceptionally weary. Dragging his feet along the bronzed grasses and heathers of the moorland, there was nowhere to stop to rest along the Edge. Finding a hollow where the wind did not blow, Robin spent the night, his reverie filled with kisses from Marion, while his loyal followers watched over him until daybreak.

There is another version of this story where Robin, drowsy from sleeping on the rocks, met the fairy folk who lived along the Edge, their shapes rain-blurred against the stone. In the liminal space between consciousness and dream, Robin overheard their chatter. The fairies were angry at first that he had dared to eavesdrop, but recognising him as a hero they warned him that Robin's nemesis, the Sheriff of Nottingham, was in hot pursuit. The next day, when the Sheriff expected to ambush Robin, he and his Merry Men were long gone.

Ghostly Goings on in Old Stubley Hall

About a mile away from the market town of Littleborough is the pretty, stone Old Stubley Hall. Now privately owned, it has pretty geometric gardens, wood carving, and original stained glass.

During medieval times, Littleborough was a centre of domestic woollen cloth production and the origins of the hall can be traced back to the twelfth century and attributed to Nicholas de Stubley. Although it cannot be proven, during the reign of Henry VII, around 1529, Robert Holt rebuilt Stubley Hall changing the structure, although it is considered the first all-brick and stone building in Lancashire.

There have been many reports over the years of ghostly activity, including sightings of Victorian staff and glimpses of a Cavalier – perhaps one of Edward's friends – within the hall. However, the strangest ghost story belongs to Ralph de Stubley, a relative of Nicholas.

It is said that Ralph fought in the Kings' Crusade, along with Richard the Lionheart. This partly successful military tour saw the capture of Saladin, the first Sultan of Egypt and Syria. However, the Crusaders failed to capture Jerusalem, which they saw as a spiritual symbol. It was during this battle that Ralph met and fell in love with Fatima, the daughter of Saladin. She played the harp and sang to Ralph. Her kindness and beauty, the swing of her hips and the unctuous scent of incense in her hair, soon enraptured the young man and the two began a passionate love affair, swearing their undying love to each other.

After the battle of Jaffa, where a treaty was signed between Saladin and Richard, the Lionheart took his men back home. Holding back tears and kissing Fatima tenderly, Ralph again pledged his love to her. He promised to return and gave her a precious diamond studded cross; a symbol of both his Christianity and love.

Three years went by. Fatima had not heard from her sweet Ralph. She was so sad that she could no longer play the tunes she used to enjoy on her harp. She then decided to take matters into her own hands. She disguised herself as a troubadour and sought passage on a ship bound for England. During the journey there was an almighty storm at night, the ship bent and creaked, the crew feared for their lives. The captain made the decision to turn the vessel into the nearest port. This ill-fated journey was bought to a close when the port they entered was rife with plague. All the crew were overcome by sickness and died, Fatima too perished. It was Christmas Eve.

On the same night that Fatima died, Ralph was due to be married to another. It was a marriage of convenience: his new wife's dowry would certainly buy his family out of the dire straits that it had found itself in. Ralph was the only person not enjoying the nuptial celebrations. He stood by one of the windows and heard the familiar sound of harp strings, playing a traditional Saracen love song. At once, he ran outside towards the sounds of Fatima's harp. He ran as fast as he could beyond the grounds of the hall into a copse of oak trees.

A handful of hours later, the wedding guests realised that Ralph was missing. They pulled together a search party. When they found him, Ralph was lying dead next to the oldest oak tree. It had started to snow, and the snowflakes covered his body, lightly dusting the diamond and ruby cross that was clenched in his hand.

On Christmas Eve, should you be in or near Stubley Hall, you may be able to hear the sweet melodies of Fatima's harp.

THE FAIRY CHAPEL AT HEALEY DELL

Near where the River Spodden bubbles, there is now a nature reserve. This area is reputed to have been the main rendezvous place of the fairy folk. According to Revd Oakley, some people believed that fairy butter, which is the sap or any other substance that oozed from trees, was a sign of recent fairy activity. Some believed that the fairies were harmless, and that these magical confabs were held to avert evil.

However, other tales paint the fairies as quite malevolent. Ralph Miller was a farmer who blasphemed against his landlord. His wife begged of him to repent but he would not. One day, Ralph fell down the valley towards the Spodden. He was met by fairies who threatened to tell the landlord what he had said, which would have meant ruination for poor Ralph. The fairies struck a bargain with the hapless farmer; they told him to throw himself at the mercy of the landlord. He was told to beg at Eleanor, the landlord's pretty daughter's feet, and to give her a token – a stone – write the name of one she loved upon it then throw the stone into the Spodden.

Ralph did as he was told; he had his farm and family to keep. He went to Eleanor who was kind and forgiving as well as beautiful. She did as she was told too. She wrote a name on the stone, walked down to the river and threw it into the glittering waters.

At once there was a disappointed cry: 'The name on this stone is not mine! And now you will pay. Maid, wife, and widow in one day, this shall be your destiny.'

Eleanor felt doomed.

Time passed, and on the day that Eleanor was due to be married she had forgotten about the curse. Her wedding day was truly wonderful. There was feasting, dancing and merriment. Sleepy and sated, the couple set off for their new marital home. On the way, they bumped into some members of a rival family, the Traffords. Taking offence at Eleanor's new husband, words were exchanged. Harsh words soon became a skirmish, and the skirmish escalated until Eleanor's new husband was mortally wounded. As he lay dying in her arms she heard the voice again: 'Maid, wife, and widow in one day, this shall be your destiny.'

It was too late. Sadly, she made her way home as a grieving widow.

Some wonder why Eleanor was treated so harshly; surely an innocent woman would not have happened upon the fairy folk? Some wonder how Eleanor broke the heart of the supernatural being. Could it be because it was with this fairy that she first experienced love with before going back to her mortal lover?

FRED: With this sad tale of thwarted love we head to bed. In the morning we take a new form of transport. One a little more daring!

LILY: Yes! We travel by canoe down the River Irk towards Heaton Park. We walk across the magnificent park – one of the largest municipal parks in Europe – and then catch the bus up Bury Old Road. Arriving at the New Inn in Radcliffe, we stop for a quick bite to eat and Fred tells stories about Radcliffe and the lovely market town of Bury.

15

FAIR ELLEN OF RADCLIFFE

LILY: Well, Fred, if you can still stand after all your canoing, the floor is yours.

FRED: The relics of Radcliffe Tower are located in Bury, Greater Manchester, surrounded on three sides by the River Irwell. It is a reminder of a once great medieval manor governed by the de Radcliffes, and later on the powerful Assheton family of Middleton Hall leased it out to local farmers.

The building itself is built of the local red sandstone. It was a manor house that was said to be one of the finest in Lancashire, its red stone catching the last rays of sunshine, making the mansion glow in the gathering dusk. Within its walls the finest ancient woodwork supported the building, with beams as strong as the old oak tree trunks from whence they came.

The tower is famous for its historical reasons, but also for an ancient ballad that applied to a Lord Thomas and his daughter Ellen. Ellen was a beautiful and much admired young woman around the local area. However, it was her stepmother's avarice that lead to poor Ellen's untimely demise.

Listen closely! The story goes like this.

Lord Thomas loved to hunt and was often out with his hounds chasing deer and other game. The venison that was caught by the Lord was enjoyed by both his family and his servants. Thomas was known to be a generous man. Things were going well for him at that time; his daughter was on the cusp of womanhood and much admired by the local lads. Indeed, word of Ellen's beauty and kindness had spread around the county. When he was not hunting or feasting, Thomas spent a lot of time prettying Ellen up, and being an attentive father and friend. She was his only joy. However, as Ellen grew nearer to coming of age, her stepmother's jealousy grew harder and crueller.

One day, while Lord Thomas was out hunting, the lady pretended to go to church. Instead, she colluded with the cook, offering him a large sum of gold to dispatch Ellen. She had decided to trick her daughter into facilitating her own demise. She found Ellen in the courtyard, making a tapestry of the autumn birds that were feeding on the trees outside. A flash of red thread here for a bullfinch or a fieldfare, sewing tiny sparkling semi-precious beads for the birds' eyes.

'Hie, dear daughter. Please do this favour for me,' said the crafty woman, 'go back and tell the master cook to dress that fair and milk-white doe.'

Dear Ellen, trusting of her stepmother, put down her work and hastened to the kitchens where she found the cook waiting for her. She did not see the evil in his eyes. She made the request that was asked of her and shrieked as the cook laid a strong, meaty hand around her neck. Shaking and shivering. Too late, Ellen realised that she had been tricked by her malicious stepmother; the milk-white doe was the secret phrase for herself! But before the cook could grab his knife to cut short the maiden's life the scullion boy cried out,

'For Christ's sake, do not make a meal of her! She is her father's only joy. Please, take my life and make your pies of me.'

'No! I will do the lady's bidding, she has promised me riches,' the evil cook retorted, 'if you speak a word of this then I will be your butcher as well.'

And with that, the cook swiftly murdered fair Ellen and sliced, diced, spiced and minced her flesh into several pies. Wrapped around what was the beautiful maiden was a shortcrust pastry that was famed to melt in the mouth.

When it was time to sit for the evening meal, Lord Thomas called for his daughter and wondered why she did not come, as she

was an obedient daughter
and never tardy. He looked
across the table at his
wife. He seemed blind to
the delicious scented and
steaming pies – the centre-
piece. His wife explained,
'Ellen has seen the light and
has gone to join a nunnery.
She will not be joining
us tonight nor any other
future night.'

'Well then,' replied the Lord, heartbroken, 'we will fetch her
back, for I shall not eat nor drink until she has returned.'

The scullion boy had been standing by the main door. He came
over to the couple and and poured out wine with a shaking hand.
It was now that he spoke up, 'Sir, oh dear sir, I fear that the last
time you will see your daughter is in the pies that your wife ordered
and that the cook has made.'

A stunned silence followed, and a black look appeared on
Lord Thomas' face.

'Sir,' continued the lad, 'Sir, I speak the truth. I offered the cook
my life instead but he would not accept it. He did accept your
lady's offer of riches.'

Now Lord Thomas ran into a rage. He incarcerated both his
unfaithful wife and the wicked cook. The lady was burned at the stake
as a heathen, and the cook was made to stand in boiling lead until his
flesh dropped off like crackling and his screams were no more.

The lord then decreed that the simple scullion boy should
become an adopted son and bequeathed him all of his land.

Now it is said that somewhere in an old and abandoned cemetery near to the hall, there was a pure white tablet with the names
of Lord Thomas and Ellen on it. Over the years, the local villagers
have associated this tablet with innocence and have broken pieces
off it to use as talismans for protection and to ward off illness.

16

THE DEVIL IN THE FIREPLACE, BURY GRAMMAR SCHOOL

FRED: When I was last in Manchester, I heard this tale from the folklorist and storyteller Simon Heywood. This story was first told by Anne Bentham, a Bury housemaid, and passed down through various ears throughout the years. It is assumed to have taken place around the seventeenth century and concerns Bury Grammar School, Old Mr Hodgson the school master, and an intellectual duel with Satan.

Bury Grammar School is a public school not too far from Bury's famous market. The school is as ancient as the borough's market trading itself. The school has existed since 1570, is said to have its roots going back to the 1570s, although it was refounded in 1727, and celebrates its founders day on 6 May, the feast of St John.

In the mid-eighteenth century, the school did not accept female pupils, just boys. And as boys will be boys there was much mischief, midnight feasting and childish mishaps. Schoolboys are curious creatures, and sometimes pranks and double-dares go horribly wrong. In this case, one cold night the lads were indulging in arcane arts and some trick of black magic summoned Satan himself out of the fireplace. When they discovered that they did not have the means to cast the Old Boy back to Hell, they did what

schoolboys normally do; they tried to hide their mistake. But the horned one was not for budging. Oh no!

Shamefaced, the boys knew what they had to do; admit their mistake to their schoolmaster, Old Mr Hodgson. But the old man had already noticed something was amiss when his wooden trencher began to spin around. He met the boys in the schoolhouse and saw their collected looks of guilt and fear on their faces. With a sigh, Mr Hodgson dismissed the boys and turned to face the Devil, who was inspecting his fingernails and looking very smug with himself.

'Yes, your amateur dark artists have called me. You know the deal, you have three chances in which you can defeat me in a battle of wits. Fail, and I shall claim your soul for all eternity.'

The schoolmaster furrowed his brow, and said, in his customary slow and precise way,

'Then the first task I shall set for you is to count the blades of grass in Castle Croft.'

With that, Satan sped away in a flash of red smoke. He travelled a quarter of a mile from the school, to the land that ran north from Bury Castle along the bank of the Irwell.

It took about an hour for the beast to complete this task, and then he returned jubilant. He had managed the first task.

'Ha!' said the evil one, 'that was too easy. The next challenge, if you will.'

The frown on the schoolmaster's forehead grew deeper, and he stroked his hairless chin. The liver spots on the back of his hand caught the light from the fire, a reminder of mortality and what he had to lose.

'Well, in that case, count the grains of sand on the School Brow.'

This area was closer to the school, and was a lot sandier than it is these days. The grains were not infinite in number; it merely took Satan fifteen minutes in which to complete this task. He returned to the fireplace likety-split, warming his hooves in the heat. This was just far, far too simple; the stupid old man has just given his soul gladly.

Old Mr Hodgson furrowed his brow a final time, and observed his wrinkled hands. In this instance, Satan felt as if he had won; the old man was yielding to his fate.

The clock on the wall ticked, tocked, the turning of time echoed in the large room. When Hodgson spoke his voice was slow, yet firm. Any sign of his old age disappeared, 'For the last task, I beseech you to count the letters in the large Bible in the parish church.'

'Ha, easy!' said the Devil, jubilant.

The parish church was attached to the school, and a huge black leather-bound Bible was there on the pulpit. With a flourish, Satan's hooves pulled open the book. However, when he tried to read the book, he found that the words blurred and danced. He could not form the sacred text with his lips, let alone count the characters printed deeply on velum. He knew then that he had been beaten by a true master.

In a rage, Satan disappeared back into the fireplace. With a crack, a large fissure appeared in the stone fireplace: a crack that could be observed centuries later.

As the years went past, generations of schoolchildren told spooky stories as to how the deep jagged line in the stone had appeared. It served as a reminder to any who fancied meddling with the occult that things could end up getting out of hand. And no one wanted to summon the Devil back to Bury!

17

THE UNSWORTH DRAGON, BURY

LILY: Fred is going to tell us the story of the Unsworth Dragon, but first I must tell you about English dragons. English dragons are a different species from that fiery, flying Welsh variety. English dragons are worms, very large worms with voracious appetites, of the genus Lumbricus Giganticus. Here's the tale.

Hund was one of the hound-clan, the Hundingas. With a lean, powerful stature, a swarthy complexion, eyes of pitch, sunken and suspicious, a long nose and heavy jowls, a perpetually mournful visage, he looked half-hound himself. Fiercely independent, Hund had departed from the main settlement at Bury with a small group of followers and some sheep and cattle to form his own Hund's Settlement, a day's journey to the south.

They had toiled from sunrise to sunset, clearing the ground for the settlement and for pasture and crops, and then tilling the soil, planting and harvesting their wheat, barley and rye, husbanding their animals. There had been couplings between man and woman, children added to their community. Hund's woman had given him one child, a boy of seven years.

Thus, they had followed the cycle of the seasons, developing their settlement, for seven years. One day, towards dusk a stranger arrived at the settlement, a woman of exquisite beauty. She wore a belted gown with tight sleeves to the wrist and an outer garment with shorter, looser sleeves, both ankle-length, made of wool of the finest quality. To show her freedom, her copper coloured hair was unbound and uncovered, falling to her shoulders, and she carried a long dagger at her belt.

The woman asked to stay for three nights and was quickly made welcome. She listened attentively to the women, deftly fended off the attentions of the men, and laughed and played with the children, especially making friends with Hund's son and winning his confidence.

The woman was careful always to remain in the shade, for she cast no shadow.

On the third day, in the gathering dusk, the woman drew Hund's son aside, to a quiet place at the edge of the settlement. She took from her loose robe a bright shiny apple impaled upon her dagger's tip and handed it to the boy with a gentle smile. The boy took the apple with shining eyes, for apples were out of season. He ate with relish, core and all, as the woman watched. For a moment her smile turned to malevolent glee, her copper hair faded to ash, her face collapsed into a cadaverous mask, then she was gone.

At the core of the apple was a tiny worm. It squirmed its way through the boy's body to the root of his spine, where it lay dormant for five times seven years. By that time Hund's son had taken over from Hund as chief of the settlement. He had Hund's hound-like countenance. He had a young son. One day the worm awoke and began to wriggle its way up Hund's son's spinal column, causing him immense torment.

In agony, Hund's son rushed from the settlement into the nearby forest. There the worm worked its will on his sinews, bones and flesh, relentlessly tearing, turning, twisting, stretching, an orgasmic ecstasy of pain, until man became worm.

Hund's son might soon have been missed, had calamity not overtaken the settlement. A dragon burst out of the forest and began at once to devour the sheep. A young shepherd rushed forward to protect his flock, waving his crook. The serpent opened his great maw and brought it down over the boy's head and shoulders. The other shepherds saw his legs flailing as he was sucked into the worm's crop.

The people poured out of the settlement with spears and axes to fight and kill the dragon, but these weapons were useless against his impenetrable hide. Many perished in the skirmish, slithering down into the creature's capacious crop.

Once the worm's desire for flesh was satisfied, he withdrew into the forest, only to re-emerge the next day, and the next. For seven weeks of seven long days the dragon ravaged the land for miles around, gorging on the people as they tended their crops and animals.

The dragon had a partiality for females. However vigilant a woman might be, the worm had a way of coming upon her unawares, burrowing through the earth and bursting out behind her. A moment too late she would turn, to be transfixed by recognition before the great maw gulped her into its gullet: the dragon bore the familial hound-face of Hund's son.

One woman, more than one, was able to flee. The serpent caught her with his tail and gathered her in his coils. He crushed her till her bones cracked, then, lifting her aloft, he let go. She fell, her eyes wide with terror, screaming and flailing, head-first down the gaping gullet of Hund's son.

From the worm's crop radiated the hot stench of blood and decaying flesh, the acrid reek of lost wives and daughters drifting across the fields and settlements.

After seven weeks, Hund's son staggered back into the settlement, naked and confused, with no notion of his whereabouts these long weeks.

Memory of the dragon evoked such horror it was rarely spoken of, and as one generation succeeded another the memory faded.

After twice seven generations, Hund's successor, also called Hund, was smitten by a strange malady making him cringe with excruciating pain, like an army of ants, he screamed, crawling beneath his skin. In agony, he rushed from the settlement into the forest. The worm had returned.

For seven weeks of seven long days the dragon decimated the womenfolk all around, sucking them into his crop in the very moment they recognised the familial face of Hund, grinding them in his gizzard. The pungent odour of death from the worm's crop reached across the landscape. After that time, Hund returned to the settlement, naked and befuddled.

After twice seven generations, the dragon returned, devastating the hamlet of Hunderwrth, then again after a further twice seven generations.

In the village of Unsworth, a young man, Thomas Unsworth, was becoming anxious about his father, Squire Thomas, who had complained of agonizing pain, like fiends with sharp fangs feasting upon his vitals, and then had suddenly disappeared. Hearing a commotion, Thomas rushed out to find the villagers scurrying around in terror of a fierce dragon which had just emerged from the forest and was gobbling up the women working in the fields before they could flee.

Several knights with manors nearby donned their armour, took their lances and swords, and rode out fearlessly to face the dragon. Alas, swords and lances glanced uselessly off the worm's tough coils. The dragon swallowed the knights whole and shat out their armour. Some knights took up their petronels and harquebuses and fired at the dragon. It was futile. Even a sustained harquebusade failed to deter the beast from his feasting.

Seeing the failure of the fusillade and fearing his father had been taken by the dragon, Thomas Unsworth devised a plan. He cleaned and primed his father's petronel. He loaded his long dagger into the firearm's barrel. He lit the slow burn match and clamped it onto the serpentine lever beside the flash pan. He donned his father's old black armour and belted on his sword. Thus equipped and attired, he mounted his father's faithful charger – which had seen many a tourney though none like this – clicked his lance into its rest, and with the petronel held firmly against his chest he cantered out like St George to fight the dragon.

He found the worm with the legs of three children slipping through his jaws. He raised his lance. He charged the dread creature at full tilt, knowing the lance would be of no avail save to provide a diversion. At the last moment he dropped the lance, just as the dragon lowered his head and opened his fetid, suffocating, slavering maw. With his right hand now free, Thomas pulled the serpentine lever to ignite the priming powder, bellowing, 'Set a serpent to slay a serpent.'

In that exultant moment, as the dagger blasted from the barrel, fatally tearing a jagged hole in the dragon's throat, Thomas looked up into his father's familiar face.

LILY: I must add a postscript to Fred's story. Mortified at being the cause of his father's death, notwithstanding the dread circumstances, Thomas Unsworth had a carved oak table made for him, in memory of his father and of the events surrounding his death.

One of the carvings portrayed St George killing the dragon; another, a coat of arms, Thomas Unsworth in black armour holding a long dagger. The main carving depicted Thomas Unsworth's late father as he appeared in the shape of the worm. Beside his father's head were carved the letters CV, which stand for *Cursus Vitae*, 'the course of life', which in this context probably means the dragon's life has finally run its course. Let us hope so.

18

THE LANCASHIRE
BOGGARTS

LILY: Now let me tell you about some more fairy folk! Boggarts, also known as bargheists, appear in many Lancashire tales, from Moston's Nut-Nan squealing in bushes to scare passers-by near Moston to the temperamental Wyreside Hall 'knocker' who was laid to rest by a priest. Indeed, it was usually by invoking the name of God or by prayer that frightened boggarts away.

Boggarts are usually malevolent creatures; however, there are tales where boggarts act like Brownies – a more helpful sprite. However, if you have a boggart in your house you must never thank it, nor acknowledge that it exists, or it will be all the worse for you if you do.

THE BOGGART OF LEVENSHULME

Levenshulme is a small village in Manchester, just north of the Cheshire border. It is a lively town with the busy A6 – an old Roman road – running through the heart of it. Many years ago, when Levenshulme smelled more of the fresh green of grass, rather than fast food and car fumes, there lived a farmer by the name of Old Daniel/Dannel.

So the legend tells, Old Daniel's farm was the envy of Levenshulme, so much so that it were rumoured that he had done a deal with the devil himself. His farm was always spick and span and he was prosperous. The reason why his dwelling was so clean, and the farm produce abundant, was due to the help of a boggart named Puck.

One harvest time, the corn had been collected and lay in a gleaming golden pile. Old Daniel was worried that the boggart may have overworked his horses and called out, 'Puck! Have you spoiled my fine beasts of burden with your work?'

As Old Daniel had acknowledged Puck's intervention in the harvest, the boggart desisted in his work as a farmhand. The next year's harvest was ruined, with dead ears of corn scattered hither and yon. The farmer sighed; he had realised his mistake.

A short time later, one spring morning, after a peaceful and fulfilling sleep, Old Daniel awoke. He stretched his arms as the

morning sunshine gleamed through the farmhouse windows. The farmer entered the kitchen. On the table was a fresh jug of milk, warm bread, and the creamiest cheese in all of Lancashire. After Old Daniel had feasted, he sighed contentedly and looked around the room. The horse brasses on the walls shone, the floor had been meticulously swept. The farmer cried out in joy, 'Thank God for you, Puck. You have provided me with such a good breakfast and I have never beheld the house to be in such glorious condition. Bless you, Puck, God bless you.'

As soon as the old man had uttered these words, a chill wind blew through the house. The icy blast was so strong that it knocked the jug of milk to the floor where it smashed to pieces, irrevocably damaged.

Old Daniel knew that he had done badly, for you must never thank a boggart, nor call to God to bless the creature. Puck had left the farmer for good.

THE BOGGART OF BLACKLEY

Boggart Hole Clough is in Blackley, just to the north of Manchester. It is not named after the other worldly creature, but after a farmhouse which stood on the site.

As one of the stories goes, once there was a farming family called the Cheethams. They were good, honest people haunted by a malicious boggart. This creature soured the milk, scared the farm animals, and drove potential business away. No amount of begging or pleading would entreat the creature to leave, nor to desist in its devilish activity. The Cheethams could not take it anymore and prepared to flee their lodgings taking a risk on a life on the road. They packed a wagon high with their belongings. Unbeknownst to them, the boggart was clinging to the bottom of the wagon, intending to travel with the family and pester them until they died.

Placing himself on the seat of the wagon, George Cheetham looked up to heaven and thanked the Lord that the family were leaving the accursed creature. But then, from under the wagon, there was a shriek. The boggart was banished by reference to God.

Another Boggart Hole Clough story is retold in a rhyme about another farmer:

> A quaint mischievous elf,
> Made the ancient farmhouse his and there had lodged himself.
> He ate the butter, drank the milk and sucked the new laid eggs,
> The milk pails up the chimney put and cracked the table legs.
> The farmer's shoes he filled with sand, often hath been said,
> Put spiders in the buttermilk and cinders in the bread.

Unlike the Cheethams, the old farmer put up with his malfeasant friend until the end of his days.

The Green Boggart

The final tale of boggarts is of the Green Boggart. He was a wicked trickster. One of his pranks was to make himself as small as a flea so that he could speak in the ears of horses, frightening them into throwing off their riders. However, the Green Boggart's malicious pranks were troubled; humans were draining the land for their animals to graze.

He travelled from Boggart Hole Clough and chanced upon a meeting with Morgana La Faye, the famed sorceress who was key in the downfall of Arthur, the greatest of all kings. It is said that Morgana later travelled to Boggart Hole Clough to tell tales of Camelot to the court of boggarts who lived deep in the woods.

Today there is lush, ancient woodland in the valley of Boggart Hole Clough. It is a magical place where you would expect the other worldly to convene.

LILY: Now we must move on for the night is drawing near. We use our handy bus ticket and jump onto the 471. While we travel Fred will tell us a rather curious ghost story.

19

THE BLOODY FOOTPRINT, SMITHILLS HALL

FRED: Bolton originated as a settlement in the moorland known as Bolton le Moors. There's a stone circle at Cheetham Close in Egerton, Bolton, which shows that people have lived in this area for much, much longer. Indeed, there are Bronze Age memorial mounds on Winter Hill – a precipice that can be seen from Blackstone Edge on a clear day.

Smithills Hall is a hidden gem in Halliwell, Bolton. It is ensconced by modern houses, yet it is a fine example of a dwelling that made a smooth transition from medieval to Tudor times. It is one of the oldest buildings in Greater Manchester and its oldest parts date back around eight hundred years ago.

The original name for the house was recorded as Smythell in 1322. Although it is now a museum, the kitchen still feels as if you can almost smell beer brewing or catch the warm scent of bread baking. The heart of the house, the great hall, was added to along the years and the building changed and grew. This would have featured laughing and drinking – the art of fine dining was to eat from wooden trenchers.

Like so many other stately homes in Lancashire, Smithills Hall has its fair share of ghostly goings on. It has white ladies, and a distressed man and woman who have been observed floating with angry purpose. But the most interesting story concerns George Marsh.

In the 1550s, the Bartons, a wealthy farming family, were the head of the household. George Marsh, a staunch protestant preacher, presented himself before Robert Barton the owner of the estate. These were dangerous times for Protestants; Queen Mary was the incumbent Royal and an avid Roman Catholic, her persecution of Protestants spread throughout England. This gave her the apt nickname of 'Bloody Mary'. In 1554, Queen Mary's wrath caught up with George Marsh when Lord Derby, the Lord Lieutenant of Lancashire, ordered Marsh to be charged with heresy if he preached in Bolton.

Instead of being sympathetic, Robert questioned Marsh about his 'heretical' beliefs; George was so incensed that he stomped his foot on a flagstone leaving a mark that is still there today. George was martyred when he was burned at the stake on 24 April 1555. It is rumoured that on this anniversary, the mark of the footprint runs with blood. His bloody footprint, now protected by a sheet of metal, is by the withdrawing room which features deep-linen fold oak panelling that shows the coats of arms of members of the family who have lived and loved in the house.

There are several things about this story that don't ring true; if one was to observe the famous dent it would lead to the presumption that George Marsh had exceptionally big feet! However, this aside, it does not account for the strange goings on in the Green Room, just upstairs of where George made his mark. The Green Room is the most haunted room in the castle, and many poltergeist hunters have remarked upon the sinister feeling and readings that they get when in that room. Indeed, even the staff today remarked that they did not like going up to the room; it is an area where there is a deep feeling that something evil was carried out in there.

FRED: We walk to the train station from the bus stop and hop on a train bound for North West Lancashire. We disembark at Wigan.

20

MAB'S CROSS TALES, WIGAN

FRED: When we came to Wigan to research the Mab's Cross tale, we found there were three terrific tales about the people who lived in Haghe Hall long ago. Lily will tell the first one, the sad tale of Magdalene Montford.

THE TRAGEDY OF MAGDALENE MONTFORT

Magdalene Montfort and her cousin William le Norreys had been boon companions since early in her orphaned childhood when she came to live at Haghe Hall. They played hide and seek in the stately rooms, high wide corridors, narrow alleyways and secret passages of the hall. They chased each other through the neighbouring woods and fields. They danced together upon the green.

As William grew towards tall manhood and Magdalene blossomed into a beautiful young woman, they frolicked together beneath the trees. He took her upon his knee and caressed her golden hair. They fell in love and promised to be true.

Ah, but William desired to follow the crusading Coeur de Lion to the Holy Land. In his naïve zeal he told his love, 'The cross must seal our marriage.'

In vain did Magdalene entreat her lover to remain within his father's walls. All the same, she was beside him with a brave face and a sinking heart as he made to mount his charger to depart.

Then, pausing, he asked, 'Let me have thy portrait which hangs in thine apartment, that before each battle I might gaze upon thy likeness and know thy blessing.'

'Nay!' she replied with fearsome foreboding, 'For know this! Should'st thou be unfaithful, my gaze would be a bitter chastisement to thee.' She kissed his lips, whispering, 'I shall be true. Now, fare thee well, my love.'

Four years Magdalene waited at Haghe Hall for her lover's return. One evening towards sunset there was an urgent clatter of hooves in the yard, and a cry, 'Make ready! William le Norreys is come ...' Magdalene's heart rose with joy and was as soon dashed down to hear further, '... with his bride!'

The whole household hurried out, eager to greet their young lord. But Magdalene hid herself in a grove of trees beside the track and watched as William approached with banners flying, his bride riding beside him.

William le Norreys was heavy hearted and solemn faced. His cheeks were pale. His lips quivered. For, as he approached Haghe Hall, he knew he must soon confront the love he had forsaken. *'Twere well I meet with her without delay*, he thought, and spurred his charger to a gallop. At that same moment, Magdalene stepped out from the trees in the failing light, to be borne down by the hurtling horse and trampled beneath its hooves.

A shudder of despair and frenzy shook William's frame as he reined in the horse, leapt from its back and flung himself down beside her, screaming in his anguish, 'My own Magdalene, forgive me!'

Her neck and bosom were torn and bloody, her body convulsed in pain. The cold sweat of death lay upon her brow. Her eyes briefly fluttered open as she uttered her dying words, 'William, have I not been true?'

Weeping, William's bride quietly knelt beside him and his dead lover and gently asked, 'Hast thou not been untrue both to she and I?' Leaning forward, she lightly and with deep compassion placed a kiss upon Magdalene's lips, her hot tears falling upon Magdalene's pale cheeks.

Far away in the Holy Land, this woman had felt a fierce passion for William le Norreys. After his capture and imprisonment, with unwavering will and ruthless resolve she had beguiled his gaoler and by means of a promise of seduction and a sharp blade saved William's life. William had felt a debt of honour to marry her, saying nought about his love for Magdalene and his pledge to her.

With the urging of his wife, William made penance for his infidelity. As a perpetual reminder, he placed the portrait which Magdalene had denied him in Haghe Hall's gallery. And in memory of Magdalene Montfort, the lost love whom he had betrayed, he raised a cross by Standish-gate, which later came to be known as Mab's Cross.

LILY: Fred will tell the next tale, of how Sir William Bradeshaghe was the saviour of William le Norreys' granddaughter and gained Haghe Hall into the bargain.

THE MARRIAGE OF MABEL LE NORREYS

It was a time of famine. William le Norreys' granddaughter Mabel was in poor estate, spending her days at the kiln baking oatcakes from what might have fed their slaughtered cattle. Her father, Hugh le Norreys of Haghe and Blackrode, was ailing and old, a poor match for the predatory knights who sought to seize his estates by legal means or foul. Not least of these was Hugh's sworn enemy Sir Robert de Holand. With no son to succeed and support him, Hugh might have paid more heed to his daughter Mabel, but he did not do so. She was abandoned to her menial tasks.

A man of the sword, Sir William Bradeshaghe saw an opportunity for himself at Haghe Hall. He cantered into the courtyard of the hall, dismounted, and strolled into the kitchen where Mabel, bent backed, was removing a fresh batch of oatcakes from the kiln. She wore a tattered and stained brown gown and wimple, and her feet were bare. She looked round in alarm at the sight of an armed knight entering the kitchen. He wore a surcoat emblazoned with his coat of arms, a *Buck Passant Guardant*, a green velvet cap, a cloak flowing to his instep and a sword slung at his waist.

'Fear not, Lady!' he said, 'I bring thee tidings. Knowest thou, thou art heir to these manors of Haghe and Blackrode? Unless those gathering wolves devour thine inheritance, as they are likely soon to do with thy father so frail.'

'Nay sire,' she replied, feeling barely reassured by his words, 'I know nought and dwell on nought day by day save surviving this famine. Withal, thy words both thrust an heritance upon me and as abruptly pluck it from me.'

'Lady, it need not be so, if thou becomest my wife. I shall chase off Robert de Holand and his wolves with my bellowing words and bright steel. With me at thy side, I shall deliver thee thine heritance, the manors of Haghe and Blackrode and all which stand and all who toil upon it, and thou shalt have thy rightful estate as chatelaine of Haghe Hall.'

Thus, marriage was made betwixt Lady Mabel le Norreys and Sir William Bradeshaghe, and within a few years, with the death of her father, they inherited Haghe Hall and all his estates.

FRED: But life was not all sweetness and roses for William Bradeshaghe and Mabel le Norreys, or Mab as he called her. Here's their tale, told by Lily.

THE TALE OF MAB'S CROSS

Strife was unremitting, not least the hostility between Robert de Holand and William Bradeshaghe, whose bellowing words and bright steel were often in action. Eventually, William joined a group of disaffected knights lead by Sir Adam Banastre to revenge themselves on Robert de Holand for being too well favoured by their overlord, the Earl of Lancaster. When Adam Banastre was seized and beheaded, William had to flee. Having had enough of fighting, he felt it time to become a pilgrim and to do penance at the Holy Places, but not before bidding farewell to his wife.

Lady Mabel led William into the gallery to stand below the portrait of the lovely Magdalene Montfort, her hair a diadem of pearls and bright curls, her eyes alight with love, her lips a promise of paradise.

'Mab, my sweet love,' uttered the brave knight, passionate tears streaming down his cheeks, 'is not this our own tale?'

'It is so,' Mabel replied, 'Like her, I shall be true. Now, fare thee well, my love.'

It was many years before news reached William that the Earl of Lancaster was executed, Robert de Holand was imprisoned, and it was safe to return. Making his way to his home at Haghe Hall, he began picking up snippets of news about what had gone on in his absence. His having been reported slain, his wife Mabel had married a knight, Sir Esmon de Neville, who now occupied Haghe Hall with a contingent of men-at-arms.

It pierced his soul to learn he had been so easily supplanted and his wife had so readily proved unfaithful. He drained his heart of compassion and filled the void with ire.

Instead of a joyous return to the bosom of his family, he now faced a fierce struggle to dislodge the usurper and win back his wife. He took the guise of a palmer – left wandering since the last crusade – wearing an ankle-length black habit and hooded cape. He carried a water flask, a small crucifix, an amulet, and a wooden rune-pin with the religious text around which the holy wars had revolved: 'If any man will come after me, let him deny himself, and take up his cross, and follow me.'

William entered Wigan town via Wall-gate, offering a palmer's blessing to the mayor's halberdiers as he passed unrecognised through the portal. Walking beneath the familiar wooden gable fronts of the houses, projecting nearly midway across the street, he made his way to the triangular marketplace to linger, gather alms, and listen to local gossip. He felt both heartened and dismayed at the tale he overheard.

At Haghe Hall, Mabel is again in poor estate, poorer even than long ago. Before his fall from grace, the detested Robert de Holand had been rewarded for his great service to the Earl with a grant of feudal lordship, by which he had forced upon Lady Mabel a husband whom he nominated, Esmon de Neville, who forces himself upon her at his pleasure.

Sir William quit the town via Standish-gate and, crossing the River Douglas by footbridge, followed a gently rising path to the higher ground by Bottling Wood, from which he could overlook his domain of Haghe House and manor and contemplate his coming campaign.

The musical beat of a great anvil drifted across to him from the smithy hard by Haghe House and convenient for its armoury. The smith was a shrewd fellow and a bold one. A humorous and inquisitive cunning lurked in the corner of his grey and restless eye. His curiosity was insatiable, his mind a chronicle of all the county's news, rumour and innuendo. Even the secrets of my lady's bower eluded not his prying ear.

'St George and the Virgin protect thee, honest friend,' said William, as he stood hooded by the entrance to the forge.

'Thanks be for thy benediction, good palmer,' the smith bellowed in reply, no hint of recognition touching his features as he waved the pilgrim to a seat and placed before him a wooden porringer filled to the brim with new milk in which oatmeal was stirred, a rasher of salted mutton, and a large cake of coarse bread.

A loud and convivial conversation ensued, gradually coming round to the subject of Sir Esmon. The smith lowered his voice, 'Rot him for a churl! Sir Esmon is cruel and greedy, grudging every man his portion, but he may be ousted yet should Sir William return.'

'Sir Esmon is no favourite with his neighbours?'

'Hang him!' replied the smith, first looking cautiously about. 'There's not a man of us but would like to see 'im and 'is men packed off tomorrow upon ass-panniers. Were Sir William alive I'd speak out wi'out fear. He were a loyal knight and true. And, 'tis rumoured to be Sir Esmon's worst nightmare, Sir William returning from t' dead on vengeance bent.

'I 'ad word th'ast heard of our late master's death, and do'st bring some token, palmer, to 'is lady?'

'Thou hast shrewdly guessed. I bear the last message Sir William sent to his lady. Thinkest thou it may be delivered secretly?'

'Save thee! Peril betides 'im who would hazard a message to my lady without 'er 'usband's leave.'

'Is the Lady Mabel in health?' inquired the stranger.

'Sorely did she grieve when tidings came of Sir William's death, but sorer still she rues 'er wedding with de Neville. Poor soul! It'd melt the nails out of a rusty 'orseshoe to 'ear 'ow she moans, when she can steal privily to 'er chamber. The knight caught 'er weeping once o'er some token that belonged to Sir William, and 'e burnt it before 'er face, beating and threatening 'er into the bargain. Lately, 'e keeps 'er locked in the gallery, chiding 'er, "Thou canst tell thine ancestors thy woes and all of their estates thou 'ast forever lost."'

Having pondered the palmer's earlier question, the smith went on, 'There is a little postern gate by which I enter th' 'all to collect what needs repair, and 'appen if I let thee by thou mightest find thy way to bear thy token to my lady.'

Entering by the postern gate, William recalled as a child exploring the narrow alleyways and secret passages of the hall. William sought out a dark, dusty, low, cramped tunnel rising steeply to a hidden latticed door into the gallery. Through the lattice he could see Lady Mabel's disconsolate frown as she paced the gallery and he hissed through the lattice, 'My Lady, it is a holy pilgrim come to bring thee words of comfort.' She looked up startled. He said again, 'My Lady, open the door that I might speak with thee.'

She sought the place from which the voice had come and heaving open the ancient, creaking door she blurted out, 'Good pilgrim, so unexpected here, where hast thou wandered?'

Bending down through the low and narrow portal he remained leaning forward with his hood over his face, 'Lady, I return from the Holy Land.'

Shivering with fear, Mabel asked the dread question, 'Hast thou heard ought there of the fate of a pilgrim knight, William Bradeshaghe, gone these ten years?'

'Thy brother, lady?' asked the palmer with apparent ingenuousness.

'My brother! Nay, not my brother!' she vehemently proclaimed, 'With shame, sire, I confess, he is my true husband, from whom death shall ne'er part me though heaven deny me for my sin.'

The pilgrim knight spoke the lady's name, 'Mabel', and with the sound the heavens rang with the joy in her heart and she collapsed into his arms.

Slowly, the lovers became aware of a rumpus in the yard. Through the tall casement they saw their retainers, craftsmen, and labourers armed with axes, smith's hammers, cudgels and scythes fixed straight on their poles, belabouring the men at arms. The all-seeing smith had mustered his motley army in minutes, since William had entered the postern gate. Then the watchers saw Sir Esmon galloping away, making his escape towards Newton.

William quickly quit his lover's arms, threw off his palmer's habit and cape, slid helter-skelter down the tunnel and out the postern gate, where the smith was ready with a fiery stallion.

Esmon drove his horse so fiercely and spurred it with such savagery, by the time he reached Newton Parke the poor beast was badly winded and William was able to overtake him.

Both men dismounted, but Esmon was quicker, rushing at William with sword high, its hilt held by both hands, while he was still turning towards Esmon and drawing his sword. Esmon might have struck a fatal blow had not the stallion been startled by the sudden action and reared up, striking Esmon on the shoulder with its hooves and knocking him sideways. By the time Esmon recovered, William was braced for combat, his ire now as cold and sharp as his sword-steel. Esmon, by contrast, agitated by his precipitate flight from Haghe Hall, unnerved by fear of William's wrath, and unsettled by being knocked sideways, proved a poor adversary and was summarily dispatched.

William walked his horse back through Wigan town. Reaching Standish-gate he found his wife. She was heavily veiled, her feet and legs bare, kneeling by Magdalene Montfort's cross.

'This is to be my penance,' she told him, 'Every week for the rest of my days I shall walk veiled and bare-footed from Haghe Hall to kneel in prayer at Magdalene Montfort's cross.' And, to this day, though the name of Magdalene Montfort be forgot, her cross is ever known as Mab's Cross.

Returning to Haghe Hall together, William and Mabel saw that the smith had been at work once more, and was ready with a welcome, for their escutcheon, the *Buck Passant Guardant*, flew again from its highest pinnacle.

WIGAN TO WALTON SUMMIT

LILY: We wake to find ourselves transported back in time to the year 1805 for the next part of our journey. We take a hackney to the southern end of the Lancaster Canal, built to carry coal from the Wigan coalfields to Glasson Dock, for shipment overseas, and to Lancaster and on to Kendal. We have hitched a ride on a coal barge.

As we pass through a Lancashire steadily becoming industrialised, Fred will tell us about the Lancashire clog, worn by Lancashire mill workers, both men and women, and by country people.

The Lancashire Clog

The Lancashire clog started out as a version of the sabot worn by Flemish weavers settling in Bolton six hundred years ago, who 'wore wode shoon all of a peece'. Us Lancashire folk took to sabots rather than having bare feet or shoes like Indian moccasins, as we'd been used to before, because they kept us dry shod in rain or snow, and we added irons to the soles and heels for the rough Lancashire ground.

Lately – we're still in 1805! – leather uppers have been taking the place of wood, 'cause they're easier to make in quantity and with rising prosperity from the growth of the cotton trade mill hands can treat themselves to leather uppers.

The Clog Maker

FRED: Here's a monologue I'll recite about making Lancashire clogs:

Owed Jim e' were a clogger, Wi' a workshop, up some steps.
Ther'll be lots o' folk a warin', those fancy clogs 'e meks.
'e cuts the soles from wooden blocks, Wi' a fancy shaped machine,
An' clever folk 'ave coed it, A clogger's guillotine.
An' when e's finished shapen' soles, An' tacked 'is leather round,
'e's ready then fer buckle on, An' pattin' toe-caps down.
A can see 'im now a shapin', Some very pointed soles,
'e sez ther for a clog-dancer, Who puts on special shows.
An' then thers bread and butter clogs, Which Jim meks by the score,
An' when ther blacked and polished up, Ther ready for the store.
But one thing's sure, ther is no doubt, For warin' on yer feet.
Yo canna beat Jim's wooden clogs, becoz ther med just reet.

LILY: Fred's just finishing his monologue as we enter Whittle Hill Tunnel. We pass through the Tunnel to our destination at the Walton Summit Canal Basin.

21

THE DE HOGHTONS OF HOGHTON TOWER

LILY: We hire horses from Walton Summit – we're still in 1805, by the way – and take a leisurely ride along lanes till we reach Hoghton Tower and canter up the long avenue to the gatehouse, where we are greeted by Sir Henry Philip Hoghton, Seventh Baronet, and escorted to the Great Hall.

FRED: Our journey around Lancashire won't be complete without this visit to one of the ancient Catholic families of the county, so I'm keen to tell you more about the de Hoghtons than you will already know: which is that when King James I made a royal visit to Hoghton Tower, the flavour and texture of a loin of beef so suited his palate that he drew his sword and pronounced, 'I knight thee Sir Loin.' The cut has been called Sirloin ever since. So, first, the de Hoghton royal lineage.

LILY: Fred's a bit obsessed by the de Hoghton lineage, so indulge him a bit. Here's his tale.

THE DE HOGHTONS

During the century following the Norman Conquest, few Normans settled in Lancashire because it was too rugged and impoverished. The land continued to be held by the free tenants – *thegns* and *drenghs* – of Anglo-Saxon and Danish blood, who had held the land before the conquest. Moreover, much of the land was waste, as the county's small population – 23,750 prior to the conquest – had been further decimated by war. There is no mention of Hoghton manor in the Domesday Book.

Gradually, however, a Norman gentry emerged and the land was apportioned to the Norman conquerors, which included the distinguished family of de Hoghton, who continue to the present day as descendants of those 'Companions of the Conqueror', Herverus and Roger de Busli.

I enjoyed long conversations with Revd Jonathan Shortt, the late vicar of Hoghton, who convinced me of the de Houghton family's Anglo-Saxon ancestry, all the way back to Earl Leofric and his wife Lady Godiva, as I have shown on the family tree.

Moreover, when I spoke to William Assheton of Downham Hall he asserted that the de Hoghtons were of royal blood; he claimed to have traced the de Hoghton lineage to the magnificent Æthelflæd, Lady of the Mercians, eldest daughter of King Ælfred the Great (849–901), and even further back to Egbert (781–838), first king of all the English, whose remains, William told me with some asperity, are heaped in a mortuary chest in Winchester Cathedral mingled together with the bones of many other Saxon kings.

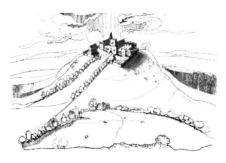

I have been able to verify Shortt's and Assherton's research for myself. The de Hoghtons do indeed have royal Saxon blood running through their veins. The de Hoghton family added this royal heritage to their pedigree when, in 1319, Sibilla de Lea married Sir Richard de Hoghton. By this marriage Sir Richard also gained Sibilla de Lea's manor of French Lea.

On the death of Sibilla's father, William de Lea, his estate of French Lea to the west of Preston passed to his son Henry de Lea. With the promptings of his mother Clémence Banastre's family, however, Henry joined the rebellion of Sir Adam Banastre. When the rebellion failed, Henry was beheaded and his sister Sibilla was able to secure the inheritance of French Lea for herself.

Sir Richard was not the first of the family to marry a Saxon, as we shall see. Turning to the de Hoghton's Norman lineage, in the early twelfth century, Hamo Pincerna allied himself by marriage to the powerful de Bussel family when he married Maud de Bussel. The de Bussels held the Barony of Penwortham, which large demesne included the manor of Hocton.

Within a generation, around 1140, an alliance of marriage was contracted between the Saxon heiress of Hocton and a son of Hamo Pincerna. It was not uncommon for the new Norman over-lords to marry into the high-ranking families they displaced, thus legalising and confirming their tenure. To add further legitimacy, this son of Hamo Pincerna adopted his wife's name of Hocton, in its Normanised form of de Hoghton, which has since endured as the family name.

There remains a mystery; the name of this son of Hamo Pincerna is unclear. William Assherton maintained it was Willùs de Hocton (born 1125), of whom some records exist. However, my research of the family tree indicates Richard (born 1125) as the first member of the dynasty to bear the name de Hoghton. As Willùs and Richard have the year of birth, it seems likely they are one and the same.

FRED: I invite you, dear listener, to study this intriguing genea-logical puzzle for yourself and see if you can solve it. Now I shall tell you tales about the builders of Hoghton Tower.

THE PEEL TOWER

Warine de Bussel, Baron of Penwortham was a disgruntled man.
His father had been a Companion of the Conqueror, and for such
great service he was awarded this pitiful, rough, wasteland of a
demesne, populated by discontented Anglo-Saxons – and for this
he even incurred a fee to the king of three knights.

With few Normans willing to settle on this unforgiving ground,
and feeling isolated, he thought it prudent to get on as well as he
could with the dispossessed Anglo-Saxon overlords, even marrying
off the lords of some Norman manors to Anglo-Saxon heiresses so
as to give his administration some kind of local legitimacy.

Warine's problems were not just about keeping a weather eye open
for Anglo-Saxon discontent spilling over into rebellion. There was a
recurring problem of Border Reivers pouring over the Scottish border
to sack, rob and burn Lancastrian towns and villages. Something had
to be done, and maybe here was an opportunity, thought Warine, for
Normans and Anglo-Saxons to join forces to fight a common foe.

He called to his castle, on a spur overlooking a ford across the
Ribble, both Norman lords and the old Anglo-Saxon barons and
thegns to talk about countering the border raids which affected
them all. He proposed the construction of a string of peel towers
similar to his own, funded by the Barony of Penwortham,
to protect the local population.

He began to suggest promising sites, such as Tulketh Brow,
when a thegn from the hamlet of Hocton spoke up, 'I knows a
reet good site, o'erlooking us little 'amlet, a gret 'ill ver' near three
'undr'd cubits a reck'n, wi' reet steep sides.'

Later, Warine de Bussel and the Hocton thegn rode side by side
to the hill at Hocton, and the Baron agreed this was an ideal site
for a peel tower.

And so, the original Hoghton Tower was built – a mount and
court earthwork castle with timber palisading and a small keep,
which served to protect the population of Hocton and thereabouts
for centuries against the incursions of Picts and Scots. As late
as 1323 Robert the Bruce cut a swath through Cumberland,

The de Hoghton Anglo-Saxon Lineage

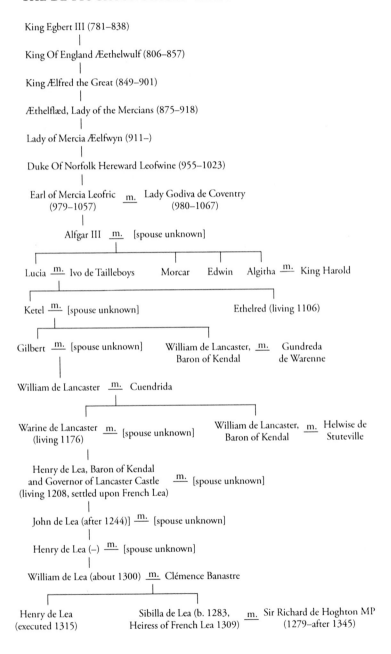

King Egbert III (781–838)
|
King Of England Æethelwulf (806–857)
|
King Ælfred the Great (849–901)
|
Æthelflæd, Lady of the Mercians (875–918)
|
Lady of Mercia Æelfwyn (911–)
|
Duke Of Norfolk Hereward Leofwine (955–1023)
|
Earl of Mercia Leofric   m.   Lady Godiva de Coventry
(979–1057)   (980–1067)
|
Alfgar III   m.   [spouse unknown]

Lucia — m. — Ivo de Tailleboys   Morcar   Edwin   Algitha — m. — King Harold

Ketel — m. — [spouse unknown]   Ethelred (living 1106)

Gilbert — m. — [spouse unknown]   William de Lancaster, — m. — Gundreda
                                    Baron of Kendal   de Warenne
|
William de Lancaster — m. — Cuendrida

Warine de Lancaster — m. — [spouse unknown]   William de Lancaster, — m. — Helwise de
(living 1176)   Baron of Kendal   Stuteville
|
Henry de Lea, Baron of Kendal
and Governor of Lancaster Castle — m. — [spouse unknown]
(living 1208, settled upon French Lea)
|
John de Lea (after 1244)] — m. — [spouse unknown]
|
Henry de Lea (–) — m. — [spouse unknown]
|
William de Lea (about 1300) — m. — Clémence Banastre

Henry de Lea   Sibilla de Lea (b. 1283,   m.   Sir Richard de Hoghton MP
(executed 1315)   Heiress of French Lea 1309)   (1279–after 1345)

THE DE HOGHTON NORMAN LINEAGE

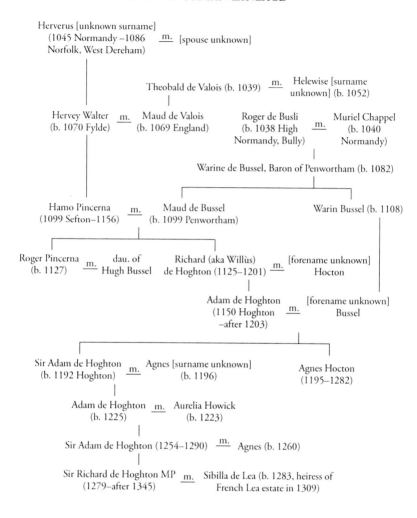

Herverus [unknown surname]
(1045 Normandy –1086 — m. — [spouse unknown]
Norfolk, West Dereham)

Theobald de Valois (b. 1039) — m. — Helewise [surname
unknown] (b. 1052)

Hervey Walter — m. — Maud de Valois
(b. 1070 Fylde) (b. 1069 England)

Roger de Busli — Muriel Chappel
(b. 1038 High — m. — (b. 1040
Normandy, Bully) Normandy)

Warine de Bussel, Baron of Penwortham (b. 1082)

Hamo Pincerna — m. — Maud de Bussel
(1099 Sefton–1156) (b. 1099 Penwortham)

Warin Bussel (b. 1108)

Roger Pincerna — m. — dau. of
(b. 1127) Hugh Bussel

Richard (aka Willùs) — [forename unknown]
de Hoghton (1125–1201) — m. — Hocton

Adam de Hoghton — [forename unknown]
(1150 Hoghton — m. — Bussel
–after 1203)

Sir Adam de Hoghton — m. — Agnes [surname unknown]
(b. 1192 Hoghton) (b. 1196)

Agnes Hocton
(1195–1282)

Adam de Hoghton — m. — Aurelia Howick
(b. 1225) (b. 1223)

Sir Adam de Hoghton (1254–1290) — m. — Agnes (b. 1260)

Sir Richard de Hoghton MP — m. — Sibilla de Lea (b. 1283, heiress of
(1279–after 1345) French Lea estate in 1309)

Westmoreland and Lancaster all the way to Preston, which he burnt to the ground, before crossing the River Ribble by the ancient ford opposite Red Scar and destroying Samlesbury Lower Hall.

According to a contemporary record, Robert the Bruce looted from Samlesbury church 'the chalice, missal, psalter, two vestments, and other property, possibly stored there in vain hope of sanctuary, including 2 wains, 18 oxen, 55 aketones, 100 lances, 30 poleaxes, 4 old saddles, 4 reins, 4 old targes, 7 brass pots, a basin, ewer, pan, bed coverlet, 2 cloth bed coverings and 2 sheets, of a total value of £18 6s 10p'.

THE ELIZABETHAN EDIFICE

In his later years, Thomas Hoghton's father, Sir Richard de Hoghton, was immune to the swirling shifts of the Tudor tide of transition. He clung to the ancient feudal customs, the old verities, the traditional Catholic doctrines, most of all he clung to the crumbling peel tower which was his abode and which he loved unreservedly. Not so his son, the Right Worshipful Thomas Hoghton. He found the three hundred and fifty year-old peel tower dank, uncomfortable and cold, with the wind whistling through the warped wainscoting.

Truth to tell, Thomas felt a surge of relief when Sir Richard died and he inherited the estate in 1559 at the age of forty-one, within a year of Queen Elizabeth I taking the throne. Thomas was thrilled to feel he was entering a golden age, a renaissance of English national pride, with naval triumph over the despised Spanish foe, international expansion, economic health, and the Elizabethan Religious Settlement bringing peace between Protestant and Catholic.

Filled with the enthusiastic spirit of the time, a spirit of enlightenment and prosperity, Thomas determined to rebuild Hoghton Tower in the Tudor style. He had a clear vision of the house which would arise on Tower Hill: 'It shall be built of millstone grit quarried from the northern flank of our hill and fashioned into well-squared ashlars. These shall be hauled in spring-less wains to the edifice rising at the summit. The house shall consist of a range of buildings, including a great hall, set around upper and lower courtyards. The buildings shall measure three hundred feet west to east and two hundred and fifty feet north to south. The house shall have a total of twenty-two hearths and as many chimneys. It shall be approached by a straight tree-lined avenue gently rising on the west side of the hill to a substantial crenellated gatehouse with a gothic arch.'

Thomas agreed a retainer with Bernard Townley, a waller and specially skilled artificer in stone, to build and finish the house, and the first stone was laid within four years of Thomas succeeding his father.

All went well until Rauff Holden appeared on the scene. A malicious and devious man, Holden had some hold over Bernard Townley, constraining him to withdraw his labour without notice from the work at Hoghton Tower and to employ them on some enterprise of his own.

Disappointed by this delay, Thomas went to see Bernard Townley, Rauff Holden also being present, gently requesting him to return to Hoghton Tower and continue the work. Townley refused. Thomas then took a firmer line, calling upon Townley to fulfil the bargain and promise he had undertaken. This time Holden replied with a sneer that the witnesses of the retainer were friends of his who would at his behest refuse to bear witness to the bargain. Thomas returned home uncomprehending of Rauff Holden's machinations and with his lewd jeers ringing in his ears.

When Thomas petitioned the Chancery Court of the Duchy of Lancaster for justice in his claim against Bernard Townley, his plea was rejected for lack of witnesses to the bargain. Thwarted in this attempt to have the work resume, he was forced to employ a different waller and stonemason.

There was a further lawsuit for the recovery of damages over the felonious removal of trees felled by Thomas for repairs and floated off on the River Darwin to Walton-le-Dale by Jane Banister and William Mason.

Despite all these delays and distractions, and to the delight of Thomas Hoghton, the rebuilding of the new Hoghton Tower was completed in 1565. Imagine how he feels as he stands in rapture at the highest eminence of his home, gazing out over the snowy peaks of the Lake District, the craggy heights of the Welsh mountains, the Lancashire plain laid out before him with its meadows and wood-lands, the placid River Ribble, the swift River Darwen plunging into a deep ravine, and in the far distance a hazy view of the Irish Sea. He has fulfilled his vision and may now relax and enjoy his new home.

THE TRAGEDY OF THOMAS HOGHTON

Alas, Thomas Hoghton had barely four years to enjoy life in his beloved Hoghton Tower. In 1569 he received some disturbing news, two ardent Catholic earls, Thomas Percy, Earl of Northumberland, and Charles Neville, Earl of Westmorland, were planning an insurrection against Queen Elizabeth in support of Mary, Queen of Scots.

When Thomas saw how this rebellion was suppressed with such merciless severity, he felt even stronger foreboding: sixty-six constables hanged for neglect of duty; eight hundred men losing their lives at the hands of the public executioner; a search for vagrants, beggars, gamesters, rogues and gypsies resulting in thirteen thousand master-less men being apprehended, most of them without visible means of support, this defect being remedied in many cases at the end of a hangman's rope.

Thomas was of two minds what to do. On the one hand, he was a known Catholic and a friend and associate of a severe critic of Queen Elizabeth, Cardinal Allen, who had been a guest at the festivities marking completion of the Hoghton Tower's rebuilding. On the other hand, he recalled his enthusiasm for the Elizabethan spirit of enlightenment and was loath to abandon his new home, which he had cause to love far more than his father loved the old peel tower.

When a friend warned him his life was in danger, Thomas felt he had no choice. He gathered together a few faithful retainers and took ship to the Low Countries. He died eleven years later. He never saw his beloved Hoghton Tower again.

FRED: Thomas' tale is told in a poem 'The Blessed Conscience' which I shall now recite. It was written by Thomas' loyal butler Roger Anderson, who accompanied him into exile in the Low Countries.

Apollo, with his radiant beams.
Inflamed the air so fair,
Phaeton with his fiery teams
The heat of wars did bear.
The day was hot, the evening cool,
And pleasures did abound;
And meads, with many a crystal pool,
Did yield a joyful sound.

This fragrant time to pleasures prest.
Myself for to solace,
I walkèd forth, as I thought best,
Into a private place.
And as I went, myself alone,
There came to my presence
A friend, who seem'd to make great moan.
And said, ' Go, get you hence.'

Alas ! good Sir, what is the cause
You this have said to me?'
' Indeed,' he said, 'the Prince's laws
Will bear no more with thee:
For Bishop Younge will summon thee;
You must to his presence;
For in this land you cannot live
And keep your consciènce.'

I am too old, I cannot ride,
What is my best to do?'
' Good Sir, here you must not abide,
Unless to church you go:
Or else to Preston you must wend,
For here's no residence;
For in this land you have no friend
To keep your consciènce.'

Then did I think it was the best
For me in time provide:
For Bishop Younge would me molest,
If here I should abide.
Then did I cause my men prepare,
A ship for my defence;
For in this land I could not fare.
And keep my consciènce.

When my ship that it was hired,
My men return'd again;
The time was almost full expired,
That here I should remain;
To Preston town I should have gone
To make recognizance;
For other helps perceived I none,
To keep my consciènce.

To lovely Lea then I me hied,
And Hoghton bade farewell:
It was more time for me to ride,
Than longer there to dwell.
I durst not trust my dearest friend,
But secretly stole hence,
To take the fortune God should send,
And keep my consciènce.

When lovely Lea I came until [i.e., unto].
And passèd by the gate,
My cattle all, with voices shrill,
As if they mourn'd my fate.
Did leap and roar, as if they had
Understood my diligence
It seem'd my cause they understood,
Thro' God's good providence.

Oh ! Hoghton high, which is a bower
Of sports and lordly pleasure,
I wept, and left that lofty tower
Which was my chiefest treasure.
To save my soul and lose the rest.
It was my true pretence:
Like frighted bird, I left my nest,
To keep my consciènce.

Thus took I there my leave at last,
And rode to the sea-side;
Into the ship I hied apace,
Which did for me abide.
With sighs I sail'd from merry England,
I ask'd of none licènse:
Wherefore my estate fell from my hand,
And was forfeit to my Prince.

Thus merry England have I left.
And cut the raging sea,
Whereof the waves have me bereft
Of my so dear country.
With sturdy storms and blustering blast
We were in great suspense;
Full sixteen days and nights they last
And all for my consciènce.

When on the shore I was arrived,
Through France I took my way;
And unto Antwerp I me hied,
In hope to make my stay.
When to the city I did come
I thought that my absence
Would to my men be cumbersome,
Though they made me no offence.

At Hoghton, where I used to rest,
Of men I had great store,
Full twenty gentlemen at least,
Of yeomen good threescore.
And of them all, I brought but two
With me, when I came thence;
I left them all the world knows how.
To keep my consciènce.

But when my men came to me still.
Lord ! how rejoicèd I,
To see them with so good a will
To leave their own country!
Both friends and kin they did forsake,
And all for my presence;
Alive or dead, amends I'll make,
And give them recompense.

But fortune had me so bereft.
Of all my goods and lands,
That for my men was nothing left
But at my brethren's hands.
Then did I think the truth to prove
Whilst I was in absence,
That I might try their constant love,
And keep my consciènce.

When to my brethren I had sent.
The welcome that they made
Was, false reports me to present,
Which made my conscience sad.
My brethren all did thus me cross,
And little regard my fall,
Save only one—that rued my loss—
That is Richard, of Park Hall.

He was the comfort that I had;
I proved his diligence;
He was as just, as they were bad,
Which cheered my conscience.
When this report of them I heard.
My heart was sore with grief,
In that my purpose was so marr'd,
My men should want relief.

Good cause I had to love my men,
And them to recompense;
Their lives they ventured, I know when,
And left their dear parents.
Then to come home straightway I meant,
My men for to relieve;
My brethren sought this to prevent,
And sums of gold did give.

A thousand marks ' they offered then,
To hinder my licènse;
That I should not come home again,
To keep my consciènce.
But if that day I once had seen,
My lands to have again,
And that my Prince had changed been,
I would not me have stay'n
'I should my men so well have paid.
Thro' God's good providence,
That they should ne'er have been afraid
To lose their due expense.

But now my life is at an end,
And death is at the door;
That grisly ghost his bow doth bend,
And through my body gore;
Which nature now must yield to clay,

And death will take me hence;
And now I shall go where I may
Enjoy my consciènce.

Fair England ! now ten times adieu,
And friends that therein dwell;
Farewell my brother Richard true,
Whom I did love so well.
Farewell, farewell ! good people all,
And learn experiènce;
Love not too much the golden ball.
But keep your consciènce!'

All you who now this song shall hear,
Help me for to bewail
The wight, who scarcely had his peer,
Till death did him assail.
His life a mirror was to all,
His death without offence;
'Confessor,' then, let us him call,
O blessed consciènce.

FRED: I was looking through some of John Roby's papers and came
across a song called simply 'Hoghton Tower', perhaps the one
mentioned in the last verse. When I showed it to the present baronet
he felt sure it's about Thomas Hoghton, so I shall sing it for you.

HOGHTON TOWER.

They bade me sing, they bade me smile, They bade my heart be gay ; They called my spi - rit forth to while The laugh-ing hours a-way.

I've sung, I've smiled: where'er my path Mirth's dazzling meteors shine; All hearts have owned its ma - gic power, And all are glad but mine.

THE CATTLE RAID OF LEA: 'THE CROW IS WHITE'

Eschewing the dank, rank reek of the old Peel Tower, Thomas Hoghton's young half-brother, also called Thomas, married Anne Kighley and made his home at the family's more commodious Mansion House at Lea.

Thomas entered into some transaction with John Singleton of Staining, whereby certain oxen, kyne and other cattle belonging to John Singleton were driven by his brother George Singleton to an enclosed pasture called the Ley, adjoining Thomas' Mansion House at Lea.

Two or more years later, with the oxen, kyne and other cattle still grazing on the Ley, a dispute arose about whom they belonged to: Thomas, John's then widow Thomazine Singleton, or his brother George.

Convinced of the rightness of her claim, Thomazine Singleton and a near kinsman of hers, William Anderton of the Forde, sought help from Thomas Langton of Walton-le-Dale and Thomas Singleton of Broughton to muster their tenants for a cattle raid on the manor of Lea to retrieve the disputed beasts.

A gang of eighty men led by Thomas Langton and Thomas Singleton met on Preston marsh, two miles from Lea, at an hour before midnight on 20 November 1589. They chose the watchword 'The Crow is White'. From Preston marsh they launched their assault on Lea armed with pikes, guns, long staves, poleaxes, swords, daggers, bows and arrows, and bills and welsh hooks.

Between eight and nine that night intelligence had been brought to Thomas Hoghton that Thomas Langton and Thomas Singleton were assembling a large group of tenants 'to do him some displeasure'.

Thomas quickly mustered thirty household servants, friends and tenants to resist the impending attack, armed with staves, one pike, one gun charged with hail shot, two pistols, bows and arrows, swords and daggers. Thomas chose the watchword 'Black! Black!'

The defenders went out of the Mansion House gate and gathered in an outhouse, close the Ley where the oxen, kyne and other cattle lay, so as to guard the beasts and be ready to take the invaders by surprise.

The raiding party arrived about an hour after midnight, dividing themselves into two companies, the first passing through the outer court of the Mansion House to reach the cattle enclosure, the second to take down the gate and hedge of the enclosure so the cattle could be driven off.

As the first company approached the enclosure the defenders sprang from their outhouse with a blast of hail-shot, gun-shot and a hail of arrows, and fell upon them shrieking 'Black! Black!' slashing with their swords and plunging their daggers into yielding flesh.

It took a few moments before the second party gathered their wits enough to realise what was happening and to throw themselves into the fray, bellowing, 'The Crow is White, The Crow is White', hacking and beating heads and shoulders with their bills and welsh hooks and staves.

In the black night of tumult and turmoil it was impossible to distinguish friend from foe, the hectic shouts of 'Black! Black!' and 'The Crow is White, The Crow is White' merging into a single scream of pandemonium and pain as demented men hacked and tore at whatever flesh was exposed in the pale light of stars.

Thomas Langton broke briefly from the fray with a frenzied shout of, 'To me! To me! The Crow is White, The Crow is White', to gather his battered and bloody force for further affray. But as they hurled themselves forward to resume the battle, they were stayed by the sight of two torn bodies slumped upon the ground. Richard Baldwin, one of the company of Thomas Langton, and Thomas Hoghton himself were slain. Thomas' head had been cloven by a poleaxe. Richard Baldwin's guts had been ripped open by an up thrust bill hook, his entrails pooling in the poor light. The fight was over.

Ann Hoghton, Thomas Hoghton's widow, gave information to justices of the peace the Earl of Derby and Sir Richard Shirburne that a great riot had been made with armour and weapons at the Lea, in which her husband and Richard Baldwin were slain. The sheriffs apprehended Thomas Langton for the offence, lying sorely wounded in his bed at Broughton Tower, likewise the widow Thomazine Singleton and others.

Special sessions of the peace were summoned the same month and twenty-four persons involved in the action were called to trial. No sufficient jurors appeared for two days, then three who did appear were challenged, and so no presentment could be made. Thus, the tale of the riotous cattle raid of Lea ended in confusion and disarray.

There was only one outcome of merit from the affair – Thomas Hoghton's widow Ann Hoghton married Richard Shirburne.

LILY: Sir Henry Philip Hoghton kindly offers to accommodate us for the night at Hoghton Tower and provides us with a meal fit for a king. In fact, it's the same menu as was served to King James I, when he knighted a loin of beef.

A DINNER FOR KING JAMES I

Sunday's Dinner 17 August 1617
For the Lords' Table

FIRST COURSE

Pullets	Goose roasted
Boiled Capon	Rabbits cold
Mutton boiled	Jiggits of Mutton boiled
Boiled Chickens	Snipe Pye
Shoulder of Mutton roast	Breast of veal boiled
Ducks boiled	Capons roast
Loin of Veal roast	Pullet
Pullets	Beef roast (Sir-loin)
Haunch of Venison roast	Tongue pye cold
Burred Capon	Sprod boiled
Pastry of Venison hot	Herons roast cold
Roast Turkey	Curlew pye cold
Mince pye hot	Pig Roast
Custards	

SECOND COURSE

Hot Pheasant, one and	three of a Dish
one for the King	Lamb Roast
Quails, six for the King	Gammon of Bacon
Partridge	Pigeons Roast
Poults	Made Dish
Artichoke Pye	Chicken burred
Curlews roast	Pear Tart
Peas buttered	Pullet and Grease
Rabbits	Dryed Tongues
Ducks	Turkey Pye
Plovers	Pheasant Tart
Red deer Pye	Hogs Cheeks dryed
Pig burred	Turkey Chicks cold
Hot Herons roast,	

FRED: On the morrow, still feeling bloated and overhung from last evening's kingly repast, we wish Sir Henry Philip Hoghton thanks and farewell and take horse through a landscape of pasture and growing crops to Walton-le Dale, where we visit my uncle at his old stone house at the top of Church Brow to listen to Lily's necromantic tale.

22

John Dee, Walton-le-Dale, Preston

Alchemy, Angels & Necromancy: Doctor John Dee & Edward Kelley

LILY: Magic has been practised for centuries. The worship of the arcane and using votives to summon the spirits has been both popular and anathema in Lancashire society for centuries, as I shall now relate.

In sixteenth-century England, science and magic were linked intrinsically. The Renaissance was a time of discovery and experimentation. Alchemy, the art of transmuting base metals into gold, was practised by many men trying to discover secrets of changing one property into another for riches or for fame.

Doctor John Dee was known as Manchester's first scientist. Dee was born around 1527 into a rich family and demonstrated an adeptness for mathematics and great intelligence. As a learned man, he wove a spell upon all he met; he rubbed shoulders with the affluent, the famous and the influential. He attended Cambridge University where rumours of his skills as a magician began – a stage trick that was so convincing the myth made the man.

Dee's golden years saw him as Queen Elizabeth's astrologer and confidante, and he strongly advocated for the expansion of the English realm. During his connection with the queen, the polymath practised scientific experiments and said that he was counselled by angels. In 1564, he published *The Monas Hieroglyphica*, a book which connected mathematics, alchemy and science. This book became one of Dee's most influential works where he believed that he was compelled to write by the spirit of God.

He devised a symbol that he believed depicted the sun at the centre as 'ruler and king'. The semicircle represented the moon as a feminine entity that reflects the light of the sun (the male). The horns that the semicircle makes are cornucopia. The cross under the image signifies the Ternary or Quarternary – the ternary is said to have a 'copulative centre'. The four right angles show the 'Octad – the threefold magic of the First fathers and the wise men consisted in Body, Soul and Spirit.' Finally, the symbol of Aries was added at the bottom of the cross to complete. The magical elements of water, earth air and fire were included. Dee claimed to be the first philosopher who had discovered this, and that the book had detailed instructions for communicating with angels for practical purposes.

However, as much as Dee professed to be under the influence of God, he grew to have a dark side. Impressed upon by Edward Kelley, another professed magician, Dee became a necromancer. Edward Kelley was a slippery character, but again one of whom was so well-connected that he was untouchable by the law. He met Dee around 1582, promising that he could help Dee connect with the angels. He also managed to convince the magician to allow him to share his wife with him; Dee was so under Kelley's thrall that he agreed. However, there are questions around whether Dee was naïve to Kelley or whether he went along in full knowledge that they were indulging in charlatan behaviour, no better than snake oil salesmen.

Whatever the case, in Walton-Le-Dale, Dee and Kelley set out on their first mission to raise the dead. It is rumoured that Dee may have accessed a Hand of Glory in order to carry out this dark art. The Hand of Glory was a gory artefact: the severed limb of a man hanged for murder. This would be the hand that did the deed and it was rendered down and used as a tallow candle. Black magic could then be undertaken as the Hand was said to open any door, perhaps even lift the veil between the living and the dead. Dee and Kelley became famous for talking to the dead in Preston and inducing them to spill out their secrets. The pair set out to the continent in order to increase their notoriety; however,

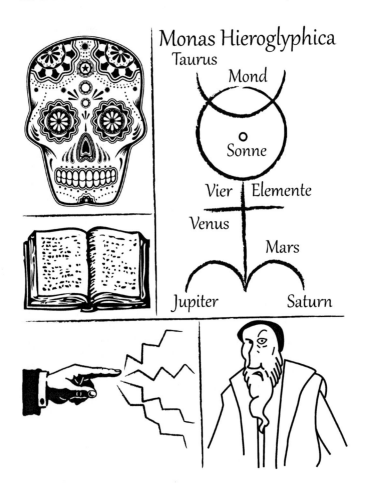

the Catholic Church caught up with them. Necromancy was frowned upon and the pair were first taken to court in San Severo in Italy. This was the beginning of the end of the men's fraternal relationship, and Kelley parted company with Dee in 1589.

Kelley travelled around Europe and was a relatively rich man. He was eventually imprisoned in Hněvín Castle to the north of Prague. He died while trying to escape by climbing out of his prison window, falling to his death hundreds of feet below, while Kelley died a rich, although imprisoned, man. In Dr Dee's later years he kept a low profile and became impoverished. He would have been anathema to the new royal King James I whose book on demonology later ended the lives of many innocent men and women accused of cavorting with the devil. No one knows whether John Dee died in 1608 or 1609, nor where his bones remain. Perhaps he was pulled into another realm by a final experiment. If we could find the philosopher's stone, perhaps one day we may find an answer.

FRED: We take horse back to Walton Summit, return our horses, and mount the 'tramcar' of the Lancaster Canal Tramroad, trying to ignore the coal and limestone dust, for this wagon was never meant to carry passengers. The Tramroad was built just two years ago, in 1803 – remember, we are still in 1805 – to link the north and south sections of the Lancaster Canal so as to let revenue traffic start flowing whilst the stone aqueduct across the River Ribble, with its many locks, was constructed. It was never built.

It's an exhilarating five-mile journey along the tramroad, across the River Ribble on a timber trestle bridge, through a tunnel under Fishergate, to the Ashton canal basin. The wagon is pulled by horses and there are also three inclined planes where the wagons are hauled up on a chain by stationary steam engines.

Quite glad to disembark from the Lancaster Canal Tramroad wagon, we walk up Fishergate to the Bull and Royal Hotel on Church Street and back to our own time for a hot bath, a welcome dinner of roast beef and potatoes, Yorkshire pudding with lots of gravy, and cabbage, and then bed.

23

THE PRESTON GUILD MERCHANT

LILY: There is a saying in the North of England, 'Once every Preston Guild', like 'Once every blue moon', because the town festival of Preston Guild only happens every twenty years. Fred's a Prestonian, so he'll tell you all about it.

FRED: Actually, my great-grandfather's friend Frank Hird wrote a well-researched piece about Preston Guild, so this is his account.

The Early Years
Granted by Henry II in 1179, the Preston Guild Merchant has existed for over seven hundred years. In the thirteenth century every town had its Merchant Guild. Preston is the only town where it still exists. In its earliest beginnings, the guild was to protect the townspeople against the tyranny of the feudal lords. These guilds laid the foundations of the English middle class.

The men of Preston had to pay King Henry II the vast sum of 100 marks, plus 700 ells of linen cloth for the privilege of the guild. An old and much dilapidated sheet of parchment called the 'Custumal or Ordinances of the Preston Guild', carefully preserved in the town archive, sets forth the benefits conferred.

Only burgesses could belong to the guild, either merchants or holders of land, and no man could be a burgess unless he had a 'burgage', a property of twelve feet frontage. The working man, 'with blue nails', 'with dirty hands', or 'who hawked their goods in the streets', received no privileges under the guild.

The origin of the guilds was trade protection. No one, not even a master of the guild, could sell any merchandise in the town without the consent of the burgesses. The custumal charged guilds with inflicting fines on burgesses for offences. Including: 'If a burgess wound another, for every hidden cut of a thumb's breadth, a fine of 4d; for every open or visible wound, 5d; plus payment to the surgeon for healing the wound.'

The custumal provided that anyone calling a married woman or a widow a particularly offensive name could be fined 3s. This sounded, alas, like open season for maids. However, anticipating Pinocchio by several hundred years, a full pardon was granted if the offender 'took himself by the nose and admitted he had spoken a lie'.

In the reign of Edward III, the guild merchant was ordered to be held every twenty years, and by the guild of 1542 the procession, which is such an important ceremony in the guild merchant, had been ordered: 'All burgesses shall be ready at the Guild Merchant to process from the Maudlands throughout the town on the first day of the Guild.'

There is no evidence of a guild being held in 1522, when war had just been declared against France; Henry VIII was claiming a tenth of the movable goods from all worth £100; the Preston merchants could not both have met the royal demand and held their guild.

The Plague Years

In the reign of Charles I the guild seems to have lost some of its ancient authority, probably owing to a visitation of the plague. The Guild Order Book records: 'That the great sickness of the plague of pestilence wherein the number of eleven hundred persons and upwards died within the town and parish, began about the tenth day of November in Anno 1630, and continued the space of one whole year.'

The terrible epidemic of plague had given strangers the opportunity of carrying on the various trades, and the guild was helpless to enforce one of the most important of its rules; in 1633 the mercers, drapers, grocers, and salters of Preston petitioning Charles I's Privy Council in this wise:

> Your petitioners at the present doe consist of very neere 80 poore persons which doe bear Scott and Lot with their neighbours. But nowe the said Burrough haveing beene visited with the plague and pestilence which infec'con continued amongst them for a whole yeare, and thereby your petitioners are altogether barred from the exercise of their trades, and so are become very much impoverished and weakened in their estates.
>
> Divers persons have sett up to employ themselves in your petitioners' several trades, having never served any apprenticeshipps to the said trades and misteries, to the general impoverishment and discountenancing of the inhabitants of the borough, which have lost a great part of their former trading and their markets are become small.
>
> Your petitioners pray, etc., Your Honors to direct some speedy course for suppression.

The Guild of 1682

A full record has been left by Dr Richard Kuerden of the 4 September 1682 celebration, and is preserved in the Heralds' College:

> About eight in the morning all the Company of Trades with the wardens of each company, in their gowns and long white rods, are ranged into two fyles and with the flags of each company displayed and a variety of music they marche regularly up and down the street singing, wayting for the Gylde Mayor's attendance. And the young men within the town, not being as yet free to trade of themselves, have a captain and leftenant of their own, their ensign being Preston town's arms, a Flagg with the Holy Lamb, and they marche and attend in like order with their drums and music.

After them marches a proper man bearing the great banner with the King's arms, and after that following in rank, the mayor's pensioners before the banner with partizans (short pikes), and those after with halberds, and then the town sergeants with their maces, the two bailiffs with their white rods, and the aldermen in their robes, and after them the Gylde Mayor with his great staff of authority, and attended on each side with nobility and gentry of the country, including myself, as well as with the gentry of the town.

The procession then passes from the mayor's house to the well-beautifyed Gylde Hall, and from here with sound of trumpet, marches to the High Cross in the market place for a proclamation that the Guild is now opened. Thence, we all repair to the church, where a learn'd sermon is preached by the Gylde Mayor's chaplain.

Divine service over, the procession is re-marshalled and marches in perfect formation to the Churchgate Barrs, where the Mayor listens to a speech made by one of the boys of the schoole. After the speech, a hogshead of nappy ale, standing close by the Barrs, is broached and a glass offered to Mr. Mayor, who drinks to the King's health, the musketiers attending firing a volley. We all drink to the King's health, several times, with several volleys from the musketiers.

The procession then marches, or rather meanders, to the Fishergate Barrs, where another schoolboy makes a speech in Latin. Another hogshead of ale is broached. As before, we all drink to the King's health, several times, with several somewhat uncoordinated volleys from the musketiers.

The procession then marches, or rather staggers, with our arms around each other to remain upright whilst raucously bellowing bawdy songs, to the Friargate Barrs. Another hogshead of ale is broached. The musketiers are now firing wildly and at random with no regard for the danger posed to the public. As before, we all drink to the King's health, several times, as dead pidgeons fall about our feet.

The procession then marches, or rather reels, totters and stumbles, with rybald bellows and boisterous badynage, back to the High Cross, where the schoolmaster entertains us with a learn'd speech in Latin, greeted by jeers, taunts and scatological catcalls from scabrously witty comedians in the crowd, followed by mocking applause. This time a hogshead of wine is broached. We all drink to the King's health, several times, whilst about us a salvo of drink-sodden musketiers greets the gutter.

Then each trade wends its way to its own hall and nobly entertains each its own society, whilst the Mayor, accompanied by the nobility and gentry, is carried to the Guild Hall where, after partaking of a sumptuous banquet with fine wine, we are regaled with store of pipes and Spanish tobacco.

The guild of 1682 was aptly summed up by a musketier, who was heard to remark as he emerged from the gutter, 'Warra day! It were right champion.'

Lord Thomas Egerton and the Guild of 1822

During the eighteenth century the celebration of Preston Guild grew more elaborate and in 1822 the festivities reached their climax, lasting nearly a fortnight. It had become the fashion for neighbouring county families to repair to Preston for the guild.

The following was the order of the procession arranged by the Marshal in Fishergate: Tanners, Skinners, Curriers and Glovers; Cotton Spinners and Weavers; Cordwainers; Carpenters; Butchers; Vintners; Tailors; Plasterers; Smiths; Gardeners; Lodge of Odd Fellows; Printers and Bookbinders; Lodge of Freemasons; Corporation, Clergy and Gentlemen.

One of the 'gentlemen' was none other than that man about town Thomas Egerton, 2nd Earl of Wilton, who now takes up the tale from his journal:

As the Marshall musters the tradesmen, trouble arises with the tailors, their pompous spokesman declaiming their allotted place in the procession as 'derogatory to our sacredly instituted profession.'

He goes on self-importantly, 'We do not intend to favour the Procession with our attendance unless we are permitted to take that situation which the high antiquity of our trade demands, and which has always been assigned to us from the Creation of the World – well, except for the last Guild, and perhaps the one before that.' He is conspicuously ignored and the tailors process regardless.

The cotton spinners escort a winding machine worked by four delightful young maidens in white cotton dresses. There is likewise a loom upon which fourteen yards of linen are made during the two days' procession, half of this being presented to Lady Derby, and the other half to the Mayoress of Preston, the ravishing Mrs Atkinson.

On the evening of the first day the Mayor gives a ball. The dresses of the Ladies are particularly splendid, uniting the very height of fashion with classical chasteness – all bustles and bosoms – which I am pleased to observe.

About nine o'clock the graceful and consummately accomplished Mrs Atkinson leads off with myself in a spritely Virginia Reel followed by my mother the Dowager Countess of Wilton and Mr E. Grimshaw. The evening then progresses from an Circassian Circle, a lively leaping dance, to a rumbustious Strip the Willow, which arouses us to such a pitch we must skip into the mayoral garden to perform a twosome Love Knot.

The second day is opened by the Mayoress' procession to church, when Mrs Atkinson again arouses the fulsome admiration of yours truly. Would that every Matins inspired such heavenly devotion and praise.

Picture for yourself the peculiar dignity and elegance with which Mrs Atkinson leads, up the central aisle of our venerable church, the magnificent train of one hundred and sixty ladies of the first distinction, the splendour of whose tightly corseted attire is equalled only by what they conceal whilst they deftly disclose.

Ah, what a sight, what a delight! There is the enchanting Miss Hoghton. There are the Miss Stanleys, those delectable daughters of Lord Stanley. Stand in line behind Mrs Atkinson, ladies, stand in line!

Races on Fulwood Moor are the chief event of the third day, at which I lose a packet. By two o'clock, when the horses start, there is a splendid display of equipages, all arrayed in new liveries, glittering in the sun like a birthday at St James'.

In the evening the Mayor gives another ball, the description of which verges upon the ludicrous by virtue of my flamboyant style:

The Mayor's Ball

This evening is attended by a most unprecedented display of fashion, particularly of the female world. The rooms are crowded to excess; to promenade is impossible. From a quarter-past nine till half-past two, the Company pours in as fast as they can be set down from their carriages. About eight hundred persons, of the very first rank and respectability in the county and neighbourhood are present.

A more enchanting spectacle it is not possible to conceive, a more agreeable and delightful society never, perhaps, met together; all is harmony, good humour, and condescension; a smile of pleasure dimples every cheek, and the careworn countenance of age is refreshed and brightened in the participation of the joyous scene.

The amusement of the evening commences with the quadrille, newly imported from Parisian ballrooms, the parties displaying their science in this elegantly intertwining square dance, to the delight of the fashionable loungers who throng the room, in their passage to and from the refectory.

The company begins to thin about 2 o'clock, but the grey tint of streaky morn had spread her changing light on the horizon before the sons and daughters of Terpsichore have ceased to trip around the magic circle of her sphere. Ah, but by then I have slipped away with the obligingly fulsome Mrs Atkinson.

Racing is again the chief occupation on the fourth, fifth, and sixth days – lots more packets lost, alas – with a masked ball on the evening of the fifth day, in a natural amphitheatre beside Avenham Walk, the masks providing convenient cover for a dalliance in a dell with the generously big-hearted Mrs Atkinson.

The second week is opened by Mrs Atkinson with a balloon ascent. The day nearly ends in tragedy; as the balloon is descending, the aeronaut, a Mr Livingstone, is thrown out. He is only saved from serious injury by landing on top of the ample Mrs Atkinson, whose abundant bustle affords him a soft and frisky fall from on high.

Concerts are the attraction on the eighth day, oratorios and a charity ball on the ninth. On the tenth, the Mayoress gives a public breakfast, at the expense of the Corporation, tickets of admission being given to all who have been introduced and are known to the

Mayoress. Some sixty young gentlemen sit down to a repast which is provided on Mrs Atkinson's most liberal and luxuriant scale.

For the townspeople and the hundreds of country folk who attend the celebrations, there is a circus in Woodcock's Timber Yard in Fishergate, Wombwell's Wild Beasts, and a Battle of Algiers Panorama, whilst Mrs Atkinson sets off firecrackers at the Bowling Green.

There is a concert in the theatre, and the stone of the New Church in the Fylde Road is laid with much ceremony in the presence of all the 'quality' assembled in the town. Oratorio and a fancy dress ball on the evening of the eleventh day – an opportunity for a final frolic to bid a full and fondly prolonged farewell to the fair Mrs Atkinson – brings the Guild celebration to a reluctant consummation.

LILY: And so, to bed.

24

THE BATTLE OF PRESTON

FRED: This morning, in her inimitable, forthright style, Lily is going to give us an account of the Battle of Preston in 1715, and how, in the words of the Duke of Marlborough, who was in overall command of government forces opposing the insurgency, 'the very beautyfull laydys of Preston and their courting and ffeasting' were the undoing of the Jacobites – also, not forgetting the 'beautyfull laydys' of Lancaster.

LANCASTER 'LAYDYS OF THE TOWNE'

Men are prey to such delusions. Our great Parliamentarians thought the best way to choose a new Head of State was to scour the blood lines of minor European royalty to find someone who professed the Protestant faith. Jacobites, on the other hand, embraced 'Mister Melancholy' – 'King Over the Water' James Francis Stuart – who according to a disillusioned supporter, Viscount Bolingbroke, 'dwelt in a maze of unrealities'.

When Queen Anne died and non-English speaking Georgie the Wurst was crowned king, the perspicacious populace exercised their sole form of political expression by pouring onto the streets in protest.

The deluded Jacobites thought this meant the people supported James Stuart. On the strength of this they staged a rebellion.

The Earl of Mar raised the Stuart standard in Scotland. In Northumberland, the rising was led by the Earl of Derwentwater, Lord Widdrington, and Mr Thomas Foster, MP for the county. Derwentwater and Widdrington being Roman Catholics feared, if either were chosen to lead the Jacobite forces, Protestant susceptibilities might be hurt. On this implausible basis, Protestant Thomas Foster was made general, despite his lack of military training or, as it turned out, acumen.

Widdrington had convinced Foster that in Manchester twenty thousand impoverished younger sons of dispossessed Civil War Royalists had been forced to seek a livelihood in commerce and were ready to take up arms in the Jacobite cause. This conviction became the guiding illusion of Foster's campaign.

Making its way south after assembling in Kelso, the small rebel army proclaimed James III as King of England at Penrith, Appleby, Kendal and Kirby Lonsdale, and in each town they collected excise duties due to the Crown and confiscated any arms and gunpowder they discovered. At Kendal, General Foster visited his godmother, Madame Belingham, who promptly boxed his ears and called him a rebel and popish tool.

The rebel army entered Lancaster in their ranks, with swords drawn, colours flying, drums beating and bagpipes playing. James III was proclaimed king. A search was made for arms, during which shopkeeper Samuel Satherwaite bestowed the only barrel of gunpowder to the town's well rather than sell it to the insurgents. A rebel Church of England minister, Mr William Paul, read Matins in the church, substituting 'King James' for 'King George' in the Book of Common Prayer.

LILY: [pauses] Much of what I shall quote, as this tasty tale unfolds, comes from a contemporary journal written by Peter Clarke, clerk to Mr Craikenthorp, attorney at law in Penrith.

Meanwhile, the 'laydys of the towne' prepared to entertain their guests. Stripping off their day clothes, they laced on tall-waisted stays, wide-fronted and narrow-backed, a loose gown of soft material with a skirt belling-out over the hips, an open-fronted bodice with richly decorated stomacher and coordinating petticoat. The overall effect was of broad hips, narrow waist, erect posture, and high, full, firm breasts, *très décolleté* as we Lancashire women say, the zenith of allure.

The women garnished their board as handsomely as their resplendent figures, as they laid out the fruits of Morecambe Bay, baked fluke, heaps of cockles and mussels, great tubs of shrimps oozing with warm butter, as well as whole baked salmon, pork chops, pheasant breasts, venison steaks, dishes of quaking pudding, shivering trifle, baked apples, fresh cream – and massive pots of tea.

Now the women were ready. In the afternoon, the 'laydys of the towne' invited the gentlemen soldiers to drink a dish of tea with them. The invitation was warmly received, and 'the gentlemen soldiers dressed and trimmed themselves up in their best cloathes for to drink a dish of tea with the laydys of this towne'. The women 'apeared in their best riging, and had their tea tables richly furnished for to entertain their new suitors' – and also to divert them.

The tea party was a singular, scintillating triumph. The gentlemen soldiers were utterly captivated by the flattering words and soft caresses of the 'very beautyfull laydys', enticing them away from all thought of conflict, but with glad hearts and full bellies they lost all appetite for affray, save for the swordplay of romance.

Until, at that climactic moment, Revd William Paul and General Foster strode in on heavy boots to declare a discourse about religion between William Paul and two papist priests to take place forthwith. Early next morning, secure in Widdrington's promise of a Mancunian Jacobite host, General Foster led his army out of Lancaster – a town easy of defence with ready access by sea to sympathisers in France and Ireland – and on the road to poorly defensible Preston.

The Lancaster women were disappointed but not disheartened by the abrupt withdrawal of their suitors. They relayed an urgent message, faster than any army could travel, via Scotforth, Ellel, Scorton, Garstang, Barton, and Broughton to the women of Preston, warning them of the approach of the Jacobite army and urging them to be ready.

THE VERY BEAUTYFULL LAYDYS OF PRESTON

Preston was the metropolis of the County Palatine of Lancaster. Many county families kept a fine house in the town, which boasted a mild climate, a picturesque location on cliffs above the River Ribble, and ease of access from the whole of Lancashire. The leading gentry of the county flocked to Preston for the 'Winter Season', which was one long round of merriment, with costume balls, charades, rowdy routs, concerts, masques and plays.

On a Wednesday evening in November, the Jacobite army arrived at Preston. The women of the town were ready. They greeted the gentlemen soldiers with open arms, even General Foster, whisking them away into a frenzied whirligig of entertainment, delight and diversion. 'The very beautyfull laydys of Preston' were even more alluring than their Lancastrian cousins, their hips broader, their waists narrower, their posture more erect and tall, their breasts higher, more full, more firm, *décolleté très généreux et plongeant*, as we proud Preston women say, the peak of feminine perfection.

> The very beautyfull laydys' ply their suitors with fine wines, sweet-meats, tasty treats, and amorous morsels. They organise masked balls where they can take their swains gently by the hand and lead them to quiet arbours for to reveal their secret pleasures.
>
> The weariness of the gentlemen soldiers' long march from Scotland falls away, as they gleefully give themselves to this glittering life of dancing and laughter, of feasting and carousing, of amusement and amours. The urgency of the Jacobite cause gives way: lethargy and lassitude hold sway. As was remarked at the time, 'The laydys in this toune are so very beautyfull and so richly atired, that the gentlemen soldiers from Wednesday to Saturday minded nothing but courting and ffeasting'.

On Friday night Lord Derwentwater received a military despatch that a government force of several thousand men under General Wills – only twelve miles away at Wigan – was about to march on Preston.

Derwentwater found General Foster upon his couch enjoying convivial entertainment. As Foster struggled to take in Derwentwater's news, his befuddled mind could grasp nothing to dislodge his belief in an illusory Mancunian mob. He waved aside the despatch and returned to his cordial couch.

Come Saturday morning, General Wills and his men were seen near Walton le Dale, close to the Ribble Bridge. Barricades were belatedly and hastily erected. As General Wills' men approached the town, Highlanders at the barricade by the church on Church Gate offered a spirited defence, which held off the government forces overnight, to the shortlived rejoicing of the defenders.

There was further skirmishing the following day, with, in all, about three hundred casualties, mostly government soldiers, but by Monday morning General Wills' forces had encircled the town and held it in a vice. To the chagrin of the brave Highlanders, who wanted to fight their way out, the Earl of Derwentwater surrendered, and Jacobite hopes lay in the dust.

'The very beautyfull laydys of Preston and their courting and ffeasting' had proved to be the undoing of the Jacobite rebellion.

FRED: Still smiling about 'the very beautyfull laydys of Preston and Lancaster and their courting and ffeasting', we enjoy a leisurely feast of a breakfast before leaving the Bull & Royal for a walk down Fishergate to the railway station and take the first train to Blackpool.

Lily: We follow the winding route through the Fylde's rich agricultural landscape with the rural village of Salwick, the attractive small town of Kirkham – originally Kirkham-in-Amounderness and a Saxon settlement, *kirk* (church) and *ham* (settlement or home) – then along the coast through Lytham and St Annes-on-Sea, passing the incomparable Blackpool Pleasure Beach to Blackpool South.

As we travel, I tell a little Lancashire tale to take Fred's mind off 'the very beautyfull laydys of Preston'.

The Old Widow Washerwoman

An old widow washerwoman of seventy married a man some years older than herself. A day or two afterwards she met the vicar of the parish, who expressed surprise at her having married again, and asked her if she had given up her washing.

'Eh, dear o' me, nowe,' was the answer. 'I've noane gi'en up mi weshin'. I fun' I couldn't wheel things out mysel', an' I'd to choose between weddin' him or buyin' a donkey!'

Fred: Hmm! From Blackpool North we take one of the old green and cream double-decker trams on the Blackpool Tramway, which dates back to 1885 and is one of the oldest electric tramways in the world. We'll go on the tram right along the promenade to Fleetwood and back while Lily reminisces about the Fylde.

25

TRADITIONS AND SUPERSTITIONS FROM THE FYLDE

LILY: My granny used to go dancing in the ballroom at Blackpool. When I was little, going to see the illuminations was a grand treat. It normally involved chips sharp with vinegar and greasy in newspaper. The rain and wind would come off the sea, but we rode the donkeys anyway. I used to love listening to my gran's friend Dot, who was from Lytham St Annes, talking about traditions of The Fylde.

Of course, first there's Lancashire Day! We used to celebrate with Goosnargh cake on 27 November. Goosnargh cake – shortbread rich with caraway seeds that stuck between the teeth. Uncle Alan used to get a bit merry and recite the Lancashire Proclamation:

Know ye also, and rejoice, that by virtue of Her Majesty's County Palatine of Lancaster, the citizens of the Hundreds of Lonsdale, North and South of the Sands, Amounderness, Leyland, Blackburn, Salford and West Derby are forever entitled to style themselves Lancastrians. Throughout the County Palatine, from the Furness Fells to the River Mersey, from the Irish Sea to the Pennines, this day shall ever mark the peoples' pleasure in that excellent distinction - true Lancastrians, proud of the Red Rose and loyal to our Sovereign Duke.

GOD BLESS LANCASHIRE.

And don't get your 'Lanky twangs' mixed up! There are three distinctive Lancastrian accents: that of Lancashire north of the Lune – a great deal of which is now in Cumbria – Lancashire between the Lune and the Ribble, and Lancashire between the Ribble and Mersey.

The Fylde is north of Blackpool, south of Lancaster, and formerly known by the rather magical name of Amounderness. This evolved from Hacmunderness in 706 BC and in the Domesday Book it was known as 'Agemundrenessa'. It is said to be named after a Norse warlord called Agmundr. It lies between the Wyre and Ribble estuaries and is known for its rich peaty soil, perfect for agriculture. In fact, the name *Fylde* is Scandinavian for 'field'.

Dot told me that the Fylde puts the 'fun' into funeral. It is said that whenever a death occurred in the Fylde the whole district was invited to take part in the funeral. Sprigs of rosemary were thrown over the coffin and the wake would sometimes descend into an orgy of drunken carousing. Fylde funerals gained a bit of notoriety because of this!

There were other strange local superstitions including the belief in omens good and evil. On a walk, if one sighted a hare, blind or lame man, a woman with dishevelled hair or even a monk approaching, it signified the approach of an unforeseen calamity; whereas visions of a wolf, the birds of St Martins flying left to right, a humpbacked man or the sound of distant thunder all heralded prosperity.

A horseshoe nailed above the stable or barn door was lucky, as long as the curve of the shoe pointed downwards. A broomstick placed across the threshold warded off witches and evil doers. Cats were banned from bedrooms as it was feared that they would 'draw the breath' of the sleeper. Shining moonbeams glimpsed through a window were capable of sending a person mad. If a child observed the moonshine, in order to prevent bad luck and imbecility, they were taught to say:

I see the moon,
the moon sees me;
God bless the priest
that christened me.

Another sign of good luck was during Yuletide. After a good wassailing, a family Yule log that burned throughout the whole of the night and the next day meant a year of good fortune. However, if the log were put out, or consumed before the end of the day, adversity was sure to follow.

As well as games such as Barley Break and hood-man blind, the festivities and gaiety around the spring were always observed. Dancing around the Maypole was a celebration that all the village partook in.

It wasn't always fun and frolics on the Fylde. There was a cruel punishment, mainly for women, called the scold's bridle which was placed over the head and into the mouth. A sharp spike prevented the poor woman from speaking. The ducking stool was another method of punishment, particularly when a woman was accused of witchcraft. The stool was fastened to one end of a pole suspended over a body of water. The woman was sat upon it, and those carrying out the punishment would swing out the contraption and plunge the victim into the water. This was done as many times as the tormentor deemed necessary.

There were various cures and charms for sickness that we would find odd today. To remove warts, one should rub a piece of stolen beef which was then buried in a secret place. Or if a bag containing the same number of small stones as warts was thrown over the left shoulder then picked up by someone else, the warts would transfer to that unsuspecting person. Finally, to ward off a sick person's death, the patient was given a pillow containing a pigeon's feather. This was believed to stave off the grim reaper.

PRESTON TO LANCASTER

FRED: Back on the train to Preston. Then we take a cab to the Lancaster Canal basin, close to the famous Tulketh Mill, built in 1905 at the height of the Lancashire cotton boom. We have hired a narrowboat for a leisurely, lock-free cruise up the canal to Lancaster.

On the way we take the two and a half-mile diversion on the canal branch from Galgate to Glasson Dock, dropping fifty-two feet through several locks.

Lily tells me the lock gates were built fourteen feet wide to allow smaller ships, like those from Ireland bringing potatoes and grain, to sail straight from the dock to the canal without having to unload their cargo onto canal barges, and likewise coal ships could sail from the canal system into the River Lune and then to the open sea.

Arriving in Lancaster we moor our narrowboat at Chancellor's Wharf where we are to spend the night. First, though, we cook egg and fried bread butties on the little grill and settle down in the cozy cabin to hear a couple of tales. Lily will tell us about the so called 'Lancashire Witches'.

26

WITCHCRAFT AND PERSECUTION, LANCASTER

Lancashire, as you may know, is said to be the most haunted county in England and is full of ghost stories from its gory past: so many have been killed in Lancaster that it got the nickname of the 'Hanging Town'. Lancashire is the county of the Pendle witches – the most famous trial of witchcraft in the world – and of the persecution of those perceived to be a little bit different to the norm.

I was told this story in a dream by Tibb, old Mother Demdike's familiar. In this vision, he appeared as a black cat, glossy as obsidian and well looked after. In this dream, we walked along the Lancaster–Leeds canal. Suddenly I realised that I could speak the language of cat, capture the sleek slink in the accent, and I heard him whisper to me in a half-meow:

Lily, by the swish of my tail, let me tell you the true tale of the Pendle witches. Living near Pendle Hill in Fence, Sabden, Barley, Blacko, Downham and Newchurch-in-Pendle. From the top of the hill and in the Bowland Valley you could hear the keening call and chatter of hen harriers as they slip through the sky.

And let me tell you of how my dear Mother, oh dear mother Demdike. How she looked after me! Her humble companion rumoured to be part-daemon. I will tell you how she came to her sad end.

I am no daemon, I prefer the term 'familiar'. Familiar for me was where the next meal came from, the soft voice that spoke soft, sweet words with flattened vowels, the wrinkled hands that stroked my soft fur. I brought her gifts, the small birds that fell from nests, mice from the fields, perhaps a butterfly that landed too near to my whiskers.

'But mother, like others, was wrongly persecuted, accused of a craft. Of curses, of herbs and potions, that although harmless to me were said to cause ill.

Tibb went on to explain about the confession of Mother Demdike – Elizabeth Southerns was her real name. Tibb was accused of being a shape-shifting demon, who changed from a small boy into a devil who offered her anything as long as she promised her soul. He was then said to have vanished for half a decade, returning as a small brown dog that tried to take blood from her arm (here, dear Tibb laughed bitterly at being accused of being such a beast).

Tibb told me of the melting-pot that was Lancaster, a microcosm of the religious and political differences that were to play out later during the English Civil War. For years, the city of Lancaster had a clandestine Catholic community which would have been in danger in a Protestant England.

When King James I took the throne, he abhorred the thought of demons and witchcraft. After the failed gunpowder plot of 1605, he led a new wave of anti-Catholicism. Indeed, it was believed that the surviving Pendle witches sought to avenge their dead, thus attaching them to further Catholic conspiracies in threatening to blow up Lancaster Castle.

Tibb and I talked about the hard life that many Lancastrians faced, early death, infant mortality. Little wonder then that if a person died suddenly the phrase 'witchcraft' followed by accusing fingers often led to people being tried and hanged for the art.

Tibb also told me about Alizon, Elizabeth Southerns's granddaughter, and how when she was out begging, she cursed John Law after he refused alms. It was said that although Law survived for a brief length of time, his face was twisted, probably by a stroke. Alison was then called to give evidence and thus the floodgates were opened.

From what the cat told me, it seemed like a mix of bad blood between neighbours, the eccentric babblings of old women and the trial at Lancaster Castle, where young Jennet Preston's childish accusations led to many innocent men and women prosecuted and killed as witches.

These unfortunates were Elizabeth Southerns (alias Demdike) Alizon Device (granddaughter of Demdike), Elizabeth Device (daughter of Demdike), James Device (son of Elizabeth Device), Alice Gray, Anne Whittle (alias Chattox), Anne Redferne (daughter of Chattox), Alice Nutter, Katherine Hewitt (alias Mould-Heels), Jane Bulcock, John Bulcock (son of Jane), Isabel Robey and Margaret Pearson.

Only one was found not guilty – Alice Gray. The rest, apart from Old Mother Demdike, were hanged on the gibbet up at Gallows Hill. Before hanging, many of the accused were kept in a deep and dirty cell in the bowels of the castle. The cell with a curved ceiling is almost homely, until you see the iron rings embedded into the stone floor. Once the door is closed it is like perpetual night in there; the eyes play tricks on one's mind in the cold mist. Demdike never got to trial; she died alone in the cell beforehand.

FRED: If that's not scary enough, Lily will tell us about the perils of the 'Oversands'.

27

THE PERILS
OF A JOURNEY
'OVERSANDS'

As John Roby said, 'To wander lost on the sands is to invite death by drowning.' Quicksand is a hazard on Morecambe Bay. Before the railway, horse-driven coaches took passengers during low tide, between Lancaster and Ulverston, travelling 'Oversands' was the fastest route to Furness. It could be a treacherous journey: the mist and sea fog can roll into the bay suddenly; a wrong turn could lead to the sudden rush and the suck of quicksand.

A macabre discovery was made in the nineteenth century; the bones of a horse and its rider, who had disappeared years before, were suddenly exposed in 'almost perfect preservation'. Until the 1820s, coach drivers traversing the sands between Lancaster and Ulverston chose their own route. These coaches risked getting caught in quicksand, or toppling over. Many horses and passengers met their doom on these trips.

Yet for the hundreds who did lose their lives over the years, the sands were a popular way to get from A to B. George Fox, the radical founder of the Quakers, was escorted across the Oversands to become a prisoner in Lancaster jail.

All is not gloomy for travellers: documents from the thirteenth century suggest there had been a Royal Guide to the Sands. These guides were on hand to assist with the journey and were knowledgeable of tide times and the ever-shifting sands of the bay.

The first official Guide to the Sands was appointed in 1536 and the post is still made today by the Duchy of Lancaster. The sands have captured the imagination of artists such as Turner in his painting *Crossing Lancaster Sands*. Poets too have been inspired by the beauty of the bay, the romance of the risk in the walk. Today, the safest way to make the journey can only be made under the supervision of the Queen's Guide to the Sands.

FRED: Before we leave Lancaster, we walk up to Lancaster Castle, which was a prison for eight hundred years. We persuade the security guard on the gate to take us into the dungeon where the poor souls accused of witchcraft were incarcerated. Deep underground we descend a flight of rough, uneven steps. It's totally black when the lights are off, even when it's broad daylight outside. The arched dungeon walls weep slime, and there are iron rings in the floor for shackling the accused.

LILY: For the next leg of our journey, we shall go back in time without leaving the present. Fred and I feel it a great privilege to have hired a Leyland Titan TD1 open-staircase double-decker bus, the Bolton Corporation No. 54, built by Leyland Motors of Leyland and purchased by Bolton Corporation in 1929. Well,

we know this is an imaginary journey, but we can dream can't we? And anyway, the No. 54 is still running today. So, climb aboard, hold very tight please, ting ting, and off we go.

LANCASTER INTO THE TROUGH OF BOWLAND

FRED: We drive slowly towards Garstang on the old north road before turning east into the Trough of Bowland. We can enjoy the drive along narrow, quiet lanes through country villages, through forests and over moors beneath gentle fells, while Lily tells us about Plague Stones. What a subject for a peaceful ride on a warm summer day.

PLAGUE STONES

In the days when the plague was a dreaded scourge, vinegar was the only disinfectant folk knew about. The ravages of the plague appeared after the First Crusade. Three thousand people died of it in Lancaster alone in the years 1348–49.

Money was believed to be a source of infection, especially in towns. The country folk bringing their produce to market during a time of plague were afraid of the townspeople's money and were also afraid to enter the town. Buyers and sellers met outside the walls, and the buyer would put their money into a hole made in a large stone filled with vinegar, and the seller would then take the money out.

These stones were called Plague Stones or sometimes Penny Stones, because a penny was most often the amount of the purchase. There were two Penny Stones at Lancaster. One was on the road from the south leading into Penny Street, the origin of its name. The other was on the north road in Ridge Lane, part of the old Roman road from Lancaster to Caton. The stone was twelve inches square, with a circular hole in the top about three inches deep and four inches wide for the vinegar. The bottom of the hole was shaped like the inside of a cup.

FRED: The bus drops us off at Higher Brock Bridge in the Trough of Bowland. We wish the driver a pleasant afternoon and take a moorland walk north, past Bleasdale Village Hall, to the Bleasdale Circle, the Gathering Circle of the next story. As we stand in what's left of this ancient wood henge, below Fair Snape and Parlick fells, we may feel at one with the Iron Age folk who inhabited this land as we listen to Lily's tale of the 'Dun Cow Of Parlick'.

28

THE DUN COW
OF PARLICK,
BLEASDALE

A dark cloud gathered over the land. Crops wilted. Grassland withered. Sheep and pigs died. The people starved.

The village folk flocked to the Gathering Circle for the ceremony of seeking wisdom from the ancestors and aid from the Earth Goddess. The Gathering Circle was on level, sheltered ground within a curve of fells, one of them Parlick. The villagers gathered within the circle's outer ring of thirty tall timber posts. The ceremony was performed by elders inside the sacred inner ring, where the cremated bones of the most ancient and wise ancestors were buried.

The elders opened the circle, calling on Serpent Spirit of the West, Wolf Spirit of the East, Bear Spirit of the North, Hawk Spirit of the South, and the Wisdom of the Ancestors to be with them in appealing to the Earth Goddess to aid the people in their plight.

As if in answer to their plea, there was a rumble in the nearby Parlick Fell, which grew to a grinding roar of great stones grating together. The earth was in travail. Parlick Fell heaved forth its progeny, a mighty beast, before the eyes of the people. It was a gargantuan cow, dun as the native stone and of the same stuff.

The ground shook beneath the Dun Cow's hooves as she trod the moor towards the Gathering Circle. She came to a stop just outside its outer ring, by a pool called Nick's Water Pot, from which she drank. With a sustained bellow reverberating across the landscape, the Dun Cow began to fill her colossal udder.

Then she tossed her great head and swung her bountiful udder, a clear signal to the famished folk. They quickly brought their earthenware pots and one by one filled them to the collared brim with the Dun Cow's copious, creamy milk.

The Earth Goddess had answered the people's plea from her own body. The community was saved. Throughout the dark time, the Dun Cow came daily to Nick's Water Pot to drink, and the people brought their pots for a share of the Dun Cow's abundant bounty. But, she only allowed each person one brimming pot. If any tried to fill another, she would shake her head and swish her tail with disapproval. Then, if the greedy milker persisted, with one quick kick she would send pots and milker flying, and gallop off, tossing her head and kicking her feet with vexation.

Sometime before, a strange woman had arrived in the village, tall and strong and dour, pulling a sled bearing a large mud pile. She told the villagers she had something marvellous to show them. She spent a day gathering straw, dry grass and ash from the village fires. Then she grabbed a hunk of thick mud and kneaded it into the shape of a hollow log open at one end, then another, until she had a collection of twelve, which she placed in the sun.

Next day, she laid layers of straw and dry grass with the log shapes between and covered the heap with ash, leaving small holes at the apex and base. She took a brand and lit the straw from the base, then sat tending the heap for a day and a night. When the hole in the top had ceased to smoke, she slept by the heap for two days. When she awoke, she carefully took the heap apart, lifted out twelve pots, and showed them to the curious villagers. They looked at the pots in wonder, turned them over in their hands, felt them with their fingers. They were amazed by the woman's magic, how she had changed a pile of mud into vessels which they saw instinctively how to use.

The mysterious woman remained in the village, though she always stayed aloof from the villagers. Soon, everyone was using

her pots, although they viewed her magical power with awe and her with foreboding. Now, her pots were being used to collect milk from the Dun Cow.

When the potter first approached the Dun Cow, she turned her broad head and glowered at the woman, her wide eyes dark with mistrust. The potter had made a vessel twice the depth and width of the villagers' pots. All the same, the Dun Cow allowed the potter to milk her, but the woman pulled on her teats roughly and with savage satisfaction. It was the same every day, the glowering cow allowed the potter to fill her oversized pot brim full, and the woman treated her with harsh and brutal disdain.

On the last day, the potter came to Nick's Water Pot in the late afternoon, where she could be alone with the Dun Cow. She placed her pot beneath the udder and began to milk. She had made this vessel with holes in the bottom. The bounteous stream of milk flowed through into a pot which could never be filled.

As her milk flowed and flowed, the cow gazed helplessly at the potter, with growing unease and distress as she became aware of the woman's enmity and malevolent design. The potter mercilessly milked on and on into the night, viciously drawing down the teats, with a widening sneer of malicious pleasure. When the udder became slack, she triumphantly stripped out the final drops. The Dun Cow's abundance was spent. She feebly kicked her heels and wandered over the darkened moor towards Parlick Fell.

The following day, when the Dun Cow failed to appear, the village folk flocked to the Gathering Circle to confer together and to consult the Earth Goddess. The elders opened the circle, calling on Serpent Spirit of the West, Wolf Spirit of the East, Bear Spirit of the North, Hawk Spirit of the South, and the Spirits of the Ancestors to join them in appealing to the Earth Goddess.

As if in answer to their plea torrential rain began to fall, lightning filled the dark sky, and there was a thunderous rumble on nearby Parlick Fell, as of great stones tearing apart. The Earth Goddess was taking back her own.

The rain ceased. The dark cloud cleared. The sun shone. The people in the Gathering Circle saw that spring was nigh. It was as if the Dun Cow had never been.

LILY: The bus is waiting for us when we return to Higher Brock Bridge. We greet our driver and climb the open stairs to the top deck. We arrive in Waddington, not far from Clitheroe, at an ancient inn with a strange name, the Dule upo' Dun, which we'll hear more about after dinner.

29

THE DULE UPO' DUN, WADDINGTON

FRED: This is the story of the Devil Upon the Dun Horse, or in local dialect 'The Dule upo' Dun', which you see depicted on the sign of this very inn.

He had been a good men's tailor, making his own patterns, doing his own cutting and sewing, keeping up with changing styles. He had fashioned woollen tunics, increasingly made to fit the body, with spangles and buttons and sometimes embroidery, linen shirts, doublets and breeches, and cloaks in woollen twill, either hooded or occasionally with fur collars. He worked hard, gave good value, built up a thriving business with the local gentry.

Then he had gone to pot, literally, as he spent more and more time in the ale house. His tailoring suffered, his business and fortune declined. Now, the only tailoring work he could get was patching and alterations. He eked out a living by selling firewood and doing odd jobs for a few pence and broken victuals.

One night in the ale house, he had spent all his money and exhausted his credit with the landlord, but had not quieted his craving for ale. He was muttering imprecations on the world as he drained the dregs from his pot, when a tall man of indeterminate age materialised at his raised elbow.

The tailor took in the man's attire at a practiced glance. He wore a tight black tunic and breeches, a plain black linen bonnet covering his hair and ears, a cloak of black sable, and black leather shoes with pointed turned up toes.

The ale house drunkards, bawds and braggarts failed to notice the stranger, their boisterous bucolic banter continuing unabated.

On a silver chain at the stranger's breast there hung an inverted silver cross inlaid with jet, matching the man's small piercing eyes, which seemed to the tailor to be piercing him to his very soul. Without a word, the tailor quickly rose and staggered from the ale house, but wending his way homeward in the winter snow he was startled to find the stranger strolling pace for pace beside him, his piercing eyes still upon him.

The stranger spoke to the tailor with quiet courtesy, 'Thy life hath been hard, but I have heard thy maledictions and have come to aid thee in thy plight. Though the world hath been cruel to thee, I bring thee word of unseen powers which can afford thee incalculable bounty. Thou hast simply to find a quiet place where thou canst recite the Paternoster backwards three times and this can be yours.'

Then, he was gone.

Throughout the next day the tailor was in torment, though he shared nothing of this with his wife. At times, his body curled with craving for the immense fortune which could be his. At other times, his vitals churned and twisted with fretful fear and anxiety when he felt the stranger's eyes were still piercing his soul. In the end, he convinced himself it could do no harm to try the stranger's charm. He found a quiet spot by the river and recited the Paternoster backwards three times. Nothing happened, save for a slight shimmering in the air. The tailor remained quite still, hardly breathing.

'So! Thou didst summon me,' spoke a quiet voice behind him. He turned. The stranger's eyes were half-closed, a slight smile upon his thin lips, his head cocked sideways, waiting. The tailor felt a rush of terror, an urgent need to flee, except that the eyes held him fast.

'What is it thou wanteth?' asked the stranger.

Inner conflict rendered the tailor speechless: one voice wanted to reply, 'Untold wealth,' and another voice, 'Nothing at all.'

Finally, the former voice managed to mutter, 'Riches!'

'Very good! Very good!' said the stranger, 'I shall grant thee three wishes, to bring thee ought thou mightst desire.'

'I thank thee,' muttered the relieved tailor, turning to leave.

'One moment!' spoke the stranger, with a restraining hand, 'there is the small matter of our contract. In return for the gift of three wishes, in seven years thy soul shall be mine.'

The tailor was greatly alarmed, 'Nay! Nay! Thou canst keep thy gifts. I want none of it.'

'Tailor! Tailor!' chuckled the stranger, 'I could take thee now, for thou hast been mine since thou didst choose to summon me. Now, slit thy finger, sign my contract in thy blood, and take my gifts and thy seven years, for it is all that thou hast.'

When the tailor returned home, in unspeakable misery, his wife had a meal of oaten bread and a small collop of bacon ready. But he was in such a state of shock he could not eat, but only sit in brooding silence, wondering if it had all been a terrible dream or an alcoholic hallucination. Thinking his behaviour was the effect of too much ale, his wife sought to lift his spirits, saying with a chuckle, 'Well, husband, if one collop'll nay content thee, I wish we'd two,' at which a second collop promptly lay hot and steaming on the dish.

The tailor stared in terror at the second collop, seeing at once that it was no delusion, then turned on his wife in a fury, 'Woman! What hast thou done? I wish thee away from here for thy foolishness.' She was gone. The second wish too was gone.

Time passed. In his wretchedness and despair, the tailor cared for nothing. His wife's vegetable garden went untended, the vegetables went to seed, his few patching and mending tasks remained unfinished, the cottage was taken over by dust, grime and vermin, he never washed. Then, one day he screamed aloud, 'Good wife! Good wife! I wish thou wouldst return,' and there she was, arms akimbo, scarlet with rage. Wherever she had been, she was in no wise happy about it.

'Bacon collops appeareth from nowhere, me whisketh away to … well, I shall not say … and now back again. Tell me what goeth on afore I take the fire iron to thee?'

The tailor told her all, amidst many heartfelt tears. After such sobering experiences, the tailor never again crossed the threshold of the ale house. He rediscovered his talent for tailoring, gradually recovering his reputation. Though he never acquired an incalculable bounty, he again became a man of modest substance.

When the seven years were nearing their end, the tailor became more and more dejected and filled with foreboding about the loss of his soul. His wife sent him to consult a hermit who lived in a cave below Pendle Hill.

After listening to the tailor's story, the hermit sat quietly for a long time, then he told him this tale:

> A younger son said to his father, 'Father, give me my portion of thy goods.' The younger son took a journey into a far country, and there wasted his substance with riotous living. He was given to feeding swine, and would fain have filled his belly with the husks the swine did eat. Then he arose, and came to his father and said, 'Father, I have sinned against heaven, and in thy sight, and am no more worthy to be called thy son.' But, his father fell on his neck and kissed him, put his best robe upon him, a ring on his finger, shoes on his feet, and killed the fatted calf to celebrate his son's homecoming, 'For this my son was dead, and is alive again. He was lost, and is found.'

The hermit continued: 'The stranger told thee thou wast already his, but this was not so. For, as in the tale, the Father cannot but forgive a repentant son. Because thou wast thus tricked into the contract, the contract is thereby rendered void.'

The tailor returned home to his wife rejoicing, and she added her own thoughts to the hermit's wise words.

At noon on the last day of the contract the tailor returned to the place by the river. This time, there was a crack of thunder and a flash of lightning, and the stranger stood before him, dressed as before, but with ravening looks and a triumphant sneer, 'Now, I shall take thy soul.'

'I thinketh not,' replied the tailor, standing his ground on shivering legs, 'because, tricking me into the contract made it invalid.'

'Invalid!' bellowed the stranger, 'Thou wast quick enough to use my gift of three wishes. I have kept my side of the bargain. Now thou must keep thine.'

'All I had from the bargain was a collop of bacon, and that I never ate,' said the tailor, following his wife's advice, 'so, it seems to me, thou art a fraud. Thou didst never intend I should gain incalculable bounty, nor do I think thou couldst ever deliver much beyond a collop of bacon.'

'What?!' screamed the stranger, his pride pricked more than he could bear, 'How dareth thee, a mere tailor, doubt my powers and deny I can keep my bond.'

At this, the figure of the enraged stranger grew to an immense height. His linen bonnet burst from his head, revealing a pair of sharp horns and long pointed ears. His pointed shoes split apart to show his cloven hooves. The buttons of his tunic popped off, exposing a livid red torso. Through the rear seam of his breeches there erupted a monstrous tail. At its hairy root it was as thick as a man's thigh. It was as sinuous as a stoat, with a vicious, barbed tip which the stranger waved threateningly before the tailor's face.

'Well,' replied the tailor, warming to the debate and thus unmoved by the stranger's changed appearance, 'as to keeping thy bond, thou didst take the first wish, the collop of bacon, even though it had been uttered by my wife, who had no part in the contract.'

'Very well,' yelled the stranger in a terrible voice, 'to show thee I can keep my bond, thou shalt have thy first wish again, that thou mayst be satisfied thou art past all hope of redemption. Then wish once more, and mind it be no beggarly desire. Wish to the very summit of wealth or the topmost pinnacle of thine ambition, for it shall be given thee.'

The crucial moment had come. Now trembling with trepidation, the tailor glanced fearfully around, then, seeing an old dun cart horse grazing quietly along the river bank, he cried in a loud voice, 'I wish thou wert riding back to thy quarters on yonder dun horse, never able to plague me again, nor any other poor wretch whom thou hast gotten into thy clutches!'

The old horse swelled with pride to twice his size. Years of toil rolled from his shoulders and broad flanks. He shook his great head, snorted loudly, and let out a mighty whinny, at which the stranger, ranting and raving with impotent rage, was whirled into the air onto the back of the dun horse, which immediately galloped off at full tilt, bearing the stranger away.

The tailor lived a long and happy life, and later a relative who inherited his cottage opened it as an inn. Remembering the story, the publican raised an inn sign depicting 'The Dule upo' Dun' in memory of his kinsman's triumph over unseen powers.

LILY: Cautiously we climb the creaky stairs to our bedchambers, where we warily peep through our windows, wondering if 'The Dule upo' Dun' might be about.

FRED: In the morning, the No. 54 bus is there to pick us up after breakfast for the short ride from Waddington to Clitheroe. We walk up to the castle, through the gateway arch, and gather in the circular walled bailey beneath the imposing tall square keep to hear some spooky tales from Lily.

30

Spooky Tales from Clitheroe

Lily: Clitheroe is in the heart of the Ribble Valley. It is a worthy jewel of a town; the castle on the conical hill is one of its most impressive features. From its height, you can see the crags of rugged rock of Pendle Hill and across the Ribble Valley. Clitheroe is chock-full of stories and history from its famous market to the mysterious hole in the castle wall. Here are a few of our favourite tales from the pretty market town.

The Castle on the Conical Hill

Clitheroe Castle is a motte-and-bailey castle built on a natural conical structure of limestone. Built in 1186 by Robert de Lacy, it is said to be the second smallest keep in England. As the civil war tore Lancashire in two, the castle was briefly captured by Parliamentary forces but was repaired in 1848. Legend has it that the devil threw a boulder from Pendle Hill and hit the castle, creating a large hole in one of the walls. (Although it's more likely that this hole was created during Civil War skirmishes.)

The Lacies were purported to have come over with William the Conqueror. It is said that as they were a refined Norman lot, they found the Saxon peasants of the area uncouth with the 'language of a Lancashire clown'. Feudalism was introduced at once and they demanded the benevolence and obedience of the local people.

However, within four generations the de Lacies became extinct and a new lord came across from Chester. Roger Fitz-Eustance married Awbrey, the sister of Robert de Lacy, and the last member of the de Lacy race. Although Fitz-Eustance took the name de Lacy, the last of the new Lacy line, Henry, died on 5 February 1310, leaving a daughter who married Thomas Plantagenet, Earl of Lancaster. This left the Earl with Clitheroe and many of Henry's other possessions were forfeit.

The honour of Clitheroe passed between many male heirs and men who married into it were – due to the law of primogeniture and the lack of women's rights – bequeathed their wife's possession.

PEG O'NELL

What should be a rather sad tale of the demise of a serving wench from Waddow Hall, has been turned into something sinister over the years.

Spanning over the River Ribble is Bungerley Bridge, near Clitheroe which is purported to be haunted by a metamorphic sprite.

The haunting comes from 'Peggy's Well', a well in the grounds of the magnificent seventeenth-century manor house of Waddow Hall next to the Ribble, supposedly named after the ghost of a serving girl who worked in the hall.

In one story, Peggy was sent out to draw up water on a wintry night, and the starless night caused the young girl to slip on the ice. She fell unconscious into the river and drowned. It is said that Peggy at first had refused to go out, fearing that she would break her neck on the slippery ice. However, her mistress made her go. After this, all maladies, disasters, sicknesses and accidents at both the hall and throughout Clitheroe were blamed on Peggy's phantom.

The story of Peg has changed and evolved over the years – as stories do. In the mid-nineteenth century it was believed that 'Peg's Night' – an occurrence every seven years – was where Peg would rise again and take a life. Animal sacrifices were made so that she would not take a human soul. There was a story of a man who was riding his horse on this fateful night, braving the crossing he took his horse across a narrow ford where there was a sudden swell of water from the river which swept up both horse and rider, taking them to their doom.

Jinny Greenteeth

A variation on the Peg story is that of water demon, Jinny Greenteeth. Many counties have similar spirits including grindylows and river hags like Peg Powler who haunts the River Tees. Lancashire's sprite is known as Jinny. She was probably invented to scare children from going in the many bodies of water in the county, saying that she'd snatch them with her bony arms, suck out their marrow and drown them alive. Jinny Greenteeth is also used to describe duckweed which could be treacherous as it looks like a solid green mat which an unsuspecting young person could walk upon and subsequently drown.

There is a tale about Jinny, that she was not always an ugly, vengeful energy. Jinny once lived on her own in a lovely little cottage in the woods near Waddington, a small village just outside of Clitheroe. She went to Clitheroe every market day and everyone would smile at her and remark how very beautiful she was. It was not long before she caught the eye of the son of a local lord who fell quickly and deeply in love with her.

Arrangements were made for the young couple's wedding; however, a day before the happy day, Jinny received a letter from her father-in-law to be. This letter informed Jinny that the wedding was off and that the son was going to London to make his life and fortune in that great city.

Jinny was broken-hearted. And it was her broken heart which began to turn her from a lovely young woman into an ugly, twisted human being. There was no love left in her heart. Her cottage went to rack and ruin, she twisted fruit and

mushrooms in her cruel knobbled fingers. She despised beauty and was jealous of other's happiness. Now nature was hurting by the ill that Jinny inflicted upon her. Nature bade her time until she could be avenged.

One sun-drenched morning, Jinny got out of bed muttering and swearing, as had become her habit. She went to the well situated some way away from her house. Reaching to place the bucket into the well, Jinny slipped. She grasped for the rope attached to the bucket but it yielded under her weight and broke. Jinny fell deep, deep down into the dark well. She could not climb out as the walls of the well were slimed with years of algae. Her clothes saturated and pulling her down, her voice hoarse from years of cursing, she could not make herself heard. Tired from shouting and fighting the weight of her clothes, she sank and died in a miserable watery grave.

But her story, of course, does not end there. Every seven years she returns. So, if you see a thicket of bramble, of nettles or weeds near the banks of the Ribble then it's Jinny in disguise. She entreats you to come closer, to take your heart and sink it deep into the depths of the Ribble. Do not heed her calls and do not go near the river, lest you end up her prey.

LILY: We stroll down into the town of Clitheroe to check in at the Swan and Royal Hotel. Ah! If you only knew what the next story will reveal about this very hostelry. After a jar or two of Jennings Cumberland Real Ale and a Mighty Mixed Royale Grill, with steak, lamb chop, gammon, sausage, black pudding, tomato, mushrooms, onion rings, fried egg and chips, we are fortified for Fred's next tale.

A SUICIDE AT THE SWAN AND ROYAL HOTEL

The friendly Swan and Royal Hotel is one of the oldest pubs in Lancashire, situated next to the castle. There has always been a building on that site since 1786, and the pub itself dates itself back to a coaching inn in the 1830s. As a hotel it has had many famous visitors from Ghandi to Winston Churchill, and the infamous dominatrix Miss Whiplash, who made the pub her campaign headquarters for her 1991 election campaign.

During the many uprisings of the cotton mill workers in the late 1800s, councilmen took over the Swan and Royal and closed many of the other bars, feeling that alcohol was fuelling the fires of dissent. In 1878, cotton workers from Manchester came to Clitheroe to meet fellow unionists. Finding many of the pubs shut, rioting commenced and windows were smashed in.

The mayor stood on the steps of the Swan and Royal and read out The Riot Act. A troop, billeted at the pub to back up the town's meagre police force, attacked the rioters, and due to the over-enthusiasm and lack of experience of the nineteen-year-old lieutenant, a few of the workers lost their lives in the fray. Feeling that things had got over the top, and having regained control of the town, the mayor vowed never again to use troops and a few of the soldiers spent the next few months just patrolling the small market town.

During the troops' stay in Clitheroe, a couple of the lads got a little too friendly with two gorgeous, young local ladies. Both couples agreed to a romantic double wedding at St Mary's parish church. However, before the wedding was due to take place, the two young men were sent off with their regiment to South Africa to fight in the Battle of Isandlwana. As history later tells us, this war against the Zulus was a disaster for England. In this futile campaign, many English men were killed in their colonial pursuit.

The two women received this news and of course were heartbroken that their lovers were no more. One of the ladies, a teenager called Anne, discovered that she was pregnant. As this would have led to scandal and shame for the family, Anne's parents instantly disowned her.

With nowhere to go, Anne wandered to the Swan and Royal Hotel where her true love had been posted and, of course, where their child had been conceived. It was in the room where they had promised themselves to each other between kisses and love-making that the seventeen-year-old took her life.

It is said that Anne's ghost had been seen on many occasions, always on the top floor of the hotel. She turns on taps, throws towels and duvets, and slams windows shut in the heat of summer. Many years ago, it was said that a child's constant crying could be distinctly heard. During the 1950s, when a major renovation to the hotel took place, the bones of a baby were found in a newspaper dating March 1879. Two months after the Battle of Isandlwana. When the bones were buried the crying phenomenon stopped.

Today, some of the regulars in the Swan and Royal still insist that Anne's sad ghost can be sensed in the establishment.

FRED: After, perhaps for some, an anxious night, and a necessarily light repast, we climb aboard No. 54, giving the driver a cheery wave, and set off down the Pendle Road to Sabden, a largish village nestling beneath the forbidding, ill-famed Pendle Hill. We alight from the bus in the village, leaving our driver to sample the delights of the Sandwitches deli, and climb Pendle Hill. We huddle together at the summit and listen to Lily's tale of Lady Sybil's desire to be a woman wise in the lore of the land.

31

LADY SYBIL AND THE MILK-WHITE DOE, SABDEN

LILY: The hanging of the Lancashire Witches, as they were dubbed, is no folk tale. It is an historic event. From our present viewpoint, it is obvious that charging these folk with the diabolical crimes for which they were condemned was – if not motivated by personal hatred and revenge – the frenzied product of superstitious times and minds. Nevertheless, it is the perception of a 'witch' as an evil, devil-possessed hag which persists, rather than as a woman wise in the lore of the land. When I tell tales of witches, it is from the latter perspective, as in the story I am about to tell.

THE LIFE OF LADY SYBIL

Lady Sybil lived in an ancient tower, on the high, wide moor, hard by the promontory of Eagle's Crag. Lady Sybil possessed charm and grace, beauty and wit. She had many suitors, not least of whom was Lord William of Hapton.

Although Lord William showed her unfailing love and devotion, Lady Sybil had no eyes for him. Her love was for the wild moor. Her greatest pleasure was to pace the hills by day, and, on such a night as this, when the moon was full and high, to stand upon Eagle's Crag, gazing upon her.

During her lonely moorland walks, Lady Sybil felt more and more drawn to becoming a woman wise in the lore of the land. She studied herbs and potions and tried them upon herself. On such a night as this, whenever the moon was full and high, she lay in the bracken by Eagle's Crag and gazed upon her, until her senses reeled and she became entranced. In her trance, she became rabbit and stoat. She became hare and harrier. She became lark and hawk, pigeon, partridge and plover. She became gorse and heather, couch grass and fern, tormentil and wild thyme. But, her greatest joy, on such a night as this, was to become a milk-white doe, a pale streak racing across the high, wide moor, or standing upon Eagle's Crag, framed against the moon and calling to her. Thus she learnt the secret lore and language of the earth.

Lord William kept watch on her from a distance, with grief and longing in his heart and growing anxiety in his guts, fearing she was losing her wits, and worse, through her practice of witchcraft she might lose her life at the end of a hangman's rope. As he kept watch, not daring to interfere, there grew in his anxious mind the idea of rescuing her from herself.

Lord William consulted an aged crone who lived in those parts. She was a healer and a wise woman, but she was also feared as a witch by superstitious folk.

'Set a witch to catch a witch,' was Lord William's maxim.

He met the crone in her herb garden, harvesting fumitory and thyme. Her face was as ancient, craggy and full of character as the harsh high moorland landscape in mid-winter. Her huge knuckles stood out from her gnarled hands. Her left leg trailed slightly as she walked around her herb garden.

When Lord William had told the crone of his fears for Lady Sybil, she invited him into her cottage, which was neat, warm and comfortable. A potion was bubbling on the open range, filling the cottage with delicate aromas of sage and sandalwood. Around the shelves were the crone's herbs of healing, many with animal names; cat's ears and mouse ear; cowslip and oxlip; chick-weed, cuckoo pint and bird's foot trefoil; hogweed and sowthistle;

toadflax and wormwood; harebell, henbit and hawkbit; foxgloves and bats in the belfry.

Lord William haggled with the crone for hours, urging her to persuade Lady Sybil to desist from her dangerous pursuit of wisdom. The crone deftly deflected the lord's cogent arguments, for they disregarded the passion in the lady's heart. The threats to the lady's life the crone treated with disdain, for they discounted the lady's will and calling. The lord's desperate offers of wealth the crone rejected with contempt, for they were a slur upon her own integrity and calling.

The crone let the lord exhaust himself of all his arguments, threats and bribes. Then she told him what he must do, 'On such a night as this, when the moon is full and high, take to the moor with your best hounds. You will start a milk-white doe from cover. Pursue her, but do not kill or harm her. When you have caught her, bind her loosely about her neck with a silken cord and lead her gently to your manor. Then sleep, and leave the rest to me.'

On such a night as this, when the moon was full and high, Lord William took his hounds to the moor and loosed them. The hounds snuffled in the bracken and gorse until they started from cover a milk-white doe, which sped away from them, a pale streak racing across the high, wide moor, leaving the hounds far behind. All save one, which the lord failed to recognise, a craggy old bitch with a game hind leg, which kept with the milk-white doe pace for pace.

With bursting lungs and aching legs, Lord William caught up with the milk-white doe as she stood by Eagle's Crag, framed against the moon and calling to her. The craggy old bitch held the doe's hind leg gently between her jaws. He threw a silken cord about the doe's neck and led her to his home of Hapton Tower. He felt she was too fair a creature to leave in a stable, so he locked her in a stately tower room hung with fine tapestries. Then he went to his couch.

Barely had Lord William sunk into an exhausted sleep after his exertions on the moor, when he was abruptly cast from couch and slumber as a great storm blew up, battering against his home, and Hapton Tower began to rock on its foundations. Worthy ancestors fell from walls, fine porcelain toppled and smashed on the tiles, pots and pans crashed onto the kitchen floors, dressers

burst open scattering family silver, chained hounds howled with fear and anguish in their kennels.

Struggling out of a tangle of sheets, Lord William made for the tower room where he had left the milk-white doe. Often he was flung against the walls, as the building rocked and tilted, or thrown down to grovel among the shards and silver, tearing his legs and hands. Bruised and bleeding he reached the tower room. As he unlocked the door, the shaking and quaking of his home subsided as suddenly as it had begun. The door swung slowly open. Instead of the milk-white doe, there was Lady Sybil, naked and at ease, quietly combing her pale tresses.

Soon after, Lady Sybil and Lord Hapton were wed. They had many children. Each day Lady Sybil walked the high, wide moor collecting herbs, often with animal names. Her family never ailed, but she had a potion or poultice to soothe and heal them. And on such a night as this, whenever the moon was full and high, her soul would soar out onto the high, wide moor, where she would lie in the bracken by Eagle's Crag and gaze upon the moon. Entranced, she became the creatures of the moor. Best of all, she became the milk-white doe, standing at Eagle's Crag, framed against the moon and calling to her.

So, whenever the moon is full and high, if you have the eyes for it, you can see her still, a pale streak racing across the high, wide moor, or standing upon Eagle's Crag, framed against the moon and calling to her. And at her heels, you can see her constant companion, a craggy old bitch with a game hind leg.

THE DEATH OF LADY SYBIL

LILY: To give you an impression of the kind of superstitious anecdotes which accrue around women who are dubbed witches, here is a tale minted shortly after Lady Sybil's death by its principal protagonist, one of her main detractors. The tale became common currency around these parts, gaining appreciation as it passed from hand to hand.

FRED: Lily launches forth again in her best Lancastrian dialect.

That Lady Sybil were allus an evil witch i' my book, allus wanderin' o'er t' moor pickin' up stuff an' lyin' down o't ground, it weren't natural, sold 'er soul to t' Devil they say. Any road, they said she were a reformed character after marryin' that Lord 'apton, Lord 'apless more like for marryin' the likes of 'er. Me, I n'er believed it, t' Devil keeps 'is own.

Any road, owd Giles Robinson 'ad me watch-keepin' 'is mill of a neet to keep out robbers and tramps and such. There I were one neet wi' just a jug to keep me company, like, when there were this commotion, a' these cats, they must 'ave come fra' all o'er, mangy critters t' lot of 'em, a' tearin' about t' mill and scratchin' and caterwaulin' an' stuff. I just wade in wi' mi cleaver what owd Giles had give me to scare of t' robbers. There were one what were limpin' a bit, a big white 'en it were, white all o'er. It were a bit slow wi't limp an' I got 'er a good smack, cut 'er front paw right off, left 'un.

I needed a good pull on mi jug after that I can tell tha', an' I get to thinkin' 'bout them cats, it weren't natural, and I reckon they was 'avin' a witches sabbath or summat an' that big white 'en were that Sybil.

Any road, once sun were up I 'ad a good look at t' paw what I'd cut off, and it 'ad a big round lump on it, like a big jewel, so I knew it must be Lady Sybil.

I took paw to 'apton Tower, went round to t' kitchen an' towd 'em, 'Ere's Lady Sybil's 'and what I cut off at owd Giles' mill, see 'ere's a big jewel on it.' Owd cook Mollie gave me a funny look, like, and told me Lady Sybil were tecken bad.

'Tha'd be tecken bad if tha'd had thee 'and cut off,' I said, but owd Mollie just called me a drunken owd fool and chucked me out. And me tryin' to be 'elpful like, nasty bit o' work, that Mollie.

Any road, Sybil were back in 'er pew come Sunday, lookin' mighty pale and no wonder, but she must've used her diabolical charms to fix 'and back on, 'cause there it were wi' t' jewel an' all, but she'd 'er cuff o'er 'er wrist so I couldn't see t' scar. I thowt, 'er must 'ave 'ad a job explainin' that to 'er 'usband.

She died soon after and I weren't surprised. Any road, parson gave 'er a proper Christian burial so 'e must've done summat to get 'er soul back from t' Devil.

Aye, it were a rum do.

LILY: We are somewhat subdued as we descend from Pendle Hill and return to Lancaster on the No. 54. Partly we are still dwelling on Lady Sybil, and partly we are reluctant for our journey around Lancashire to end. However, on the train journey to Liverpool Lime Street and back to Ormskirk, our hearts lift as we recall and recite our Lancashire Proclamation:

> Know ye also, and rejoice, that by virtue of Her Majesty's County Palatine of Lancaster, the citizens of the Hundreds of Lonsdale, North and South of the Sands, Amounderness, Leyland, Blackburn, Salford and West Derby are forever entitled to style themselves Lancastrians. Throughout the County Palatine, from the Furness Fells to the River Mersey, from the Irish Sea to the Pennines, this day shall ever mark the peoples' pleasure in that excellent distinction – true Lancastrians, proud of the Red Rose and loyal to our Sovereign Duke.
>
> GOD BLESS LANCELOT'S SHIRE.

FRED: We pick up our horses from the livery stables, and walk them through quiet lanes to Southport, where our journey began. There, we bid each and every one a fond farewell and ride away on horseback, to the south, the north, the east, and mysteriously cantering over the sands to the west.

NOTES ON
THE TALES

SIR LANCELOT AND SIR TARQUIN, MARTIN MERE

Sources:
Roby, John (1872), Volume I
This tale is largely based on John Roby's quotation from a pamphlet by a certain Dr Hibbert. As it was so superbly and expressively written, the present authors could not forbear to plagiarise many of his words, and offer this story as a tribute to the said Dr Hibbert.

THE EAGLE AND CHILD, PARBOLD, ORMSKIRK

Sources:
Harland, John & Wilkinson, T.T. (1873)
Roby, John (1872)
According to Harland & Wilkinson: 'A legend of the eagle and child is as old as the time of King Alfred, several centuries earlier than the time of the de Lathoms, "One day as Alfred was hunting in a wood, he heard the cry of a little infant in a tree, and ordered his huntsmen to examine the place. They ascended the branches, and found at the top, in an eagle's nest, a beautiful child dressed in purple, with golden bracelets

(the marks of nobility) on his arms. The King had him brought down and baptized and well educated. From the accident he named the foundling Nestingum. His grandson's daughter is said to have been one of the ladies for whom Edgar indulged an improper passion.'"

They suggest Nestingum and Edgar are one and the same, and continue, 'If for Edgar we read Oscital, the Danish prince, this would complete the parallel with the Lancashire tradition.'

The authors owe half a nod to John Roby for his inspiring account of the joust between Sir John and the Admiral of Hainault.

THE DEVIL'S WALL, AUGHTON, ORMSKIRK

Sources:

Fishwick and Ditchfield (1909)

Landreth, Peter (1841)

The bare bones of the story, according to Fishwick and Ditchfield: 'In Aughton, immediately outside Ormskirk, are Cleives (cliffs) Hills, The Devil's Wall, with its curious tradition of the Ormskirk man who outwitted the devil himself.'

You can search for the Devil's Wall in a field north of Gaw Hill. The place where the third load of sand was dumped is now called Shirdley Hill, an oasis of sand in the middle of the moss.

TALES OF BEWSEY HALL, WARRINGTON

Sources:

Hird, Frank (1912), Volume I, p. 49

Roby, John (1872), Volume II, p. 69

Sir John Boteler's ancestor, Richard Pincerna, as butler to the Earl of Chester, had in 1158 taken the name of his office, *pincerna* being Latin for 'butler'. The name was subsequently changed to the English 'Boteler'.

A later ancestor, Sir William Boteler, in 1354 built St Elphin's parish church, Warrington, where Sir John and Lady Margaret are buried. Burial of the 'negro footman' in the same grave is, alas, a folk tale, but when you visit St Elphin's parish church, look for his image on the Boteler tomb.

Lady Margaret went on to marry Lord Henry Grey of Codnor, possibly to protect herself and Tom from their enemies. She commenced a prosecution against Sir John's murderers, but Lord Grey, possibly through intimidation, exercised a husband's right at that time to declare her suit void.

You can visit the excavations of the priory of the Hermit Friars of St Augustine, at Norton Priory, near Runcorn, Cheshire.

THE SONG OF WARRIKIN FAIR, WARRINGTON

Source:
Hird, Frank (1912).
The ballad Warrikin Fair can be sung, more or less, to the tune, 'To market, to market, to buy a fat pig.'

Here is the ballad in present day English, though it loses much in translation. We have kept 'hoo', meaning 'she' and 'th'' for the.

Now, all you good gentlefolk, and you who tarry,
I'll tell you how Gilbert Scott sold his mare Barry;
He sold his mare Barry at Warrikin fair,
But when he'll be paid, he knows not, I'll swear.

So when he came home, and told his wife Grace,
Hoo took up a big stick, and swat him o'er th' face,
Hoo pushed him o' th' hillock, and he fell with a whack,
That he thought would well-nigh have broken his back.

'O wife,' quoth he, 'if thou'll let me but rise,
I'll give thee all th' light, wench, in me that lies.'
'Thou idiot,' quoth hoo, 'but where does he dwell?'
'By our Lady,' quoth he, 'that I cannot tell.'

'I took him for to be some gentleman's son,
For he spent two pence on me, when he had done;
And he gave me a luncheon o' dainty eel pie,
And by th' hand did he shake me most lovingly.'

Then Grace hoo dresséd her neatly and fine,
And to Warrikin went o' Wednesday betimes;
And there, too, hoo stayed for five market days,
Till th' man with th' mare come to Randle Shay's.

And as hoo were resting one day in her room,
Hoo spied th' man a-riding th' mare into the town;
Then bounce goes her heart, and hoo were so agape,
That out o' th' winder hoo would like for to leap.

Hoo stamped and hoo stared, and down stairs hoo run
With her heart in her hand, and her wind well-nigh gone;
Her head-gear flew off, and so did her band;
Hoo stamped and hoo stared, as if hoo had bin mad,

To Randle's hoo hied, and hoo heaved up the latch,
Afore th' man had tied th' mare properly to th' post.
'My good man,' quoth hoo, 'Gilbert greets you right merry
And begs that you'll send him th' money for Barry,'

'Oh, money,' quoth he, 'that cannot I spare.'
'By our Lady,' quoth hoo, 'then I'll have th' mare.'
Hoo pulled and hoo thumped him shame to be seen,
'Thou hangman,' quoth hoo, 'I'll put out thy eyes.

'I'll make thee a numskull, I'll bet thee a groat;
I'll either have th' money, or put out thy throat;
So between them they made such a wearisome din,
That to make them at peace, Randle Shay did come in.

'Come, fie, aunty Grace; come, fie, and have done;
You shall have th' mare, or th' money, whether you won.'
So Grace gets th' money, and homewards hoo has gone;
But hoo keeps it herself and gives Gilbert Scott none.

MANCHESTER BATTLES

The following texts were used for these:
Palmer, John, *History of the Siege of Manchester by the King's Forces Under the Command of Lord Strange 1642* (Manchester: John Leigh, 1822)
Wood, J., *The Story of Manchester* (London: T. Werner Laurie Ltd, 1915)

TALES FROM THE BOROUGH OF ROCHDALE

The cheeky description of the Rochdale accent is taken from:
J. Aiken, *A Description of the Country from thirty to forty miles around Manchester* (London: John Stockdale, 1795)

THE UNSWORTH DRAGON, BURY

Sources:
Harland, John & Wilkinson, T.T. (1873), page 63
Hird, Frank (1912), Volume I, page 104

Discussing stories of English dragons, Harland & Wilkinson tell us, 'There is a singular circumstance connected with these dragon stories. It is that of the frequent use of sacred and mystic numbers in the narratives, and this supports the conjecture that they are allegorical in their nature.' They refer to the Dragon of Wantley with its seven heads and twice seven eyes eating up three children. In the above story, we have remained faithful to this singular circumstance and used sacred and mystic numbers throughout.

THE LANCASHIRE BOGGARTS

The following texts were used:
Bowker, James, *Goblin Tales of Lancashire,* pp. 131–9 in Westwood & Simpson, *Lore of the* Land, p 401, 1883
Eyre, Kathleen, *Lancashire Ghosts* (Clapham: The Dales Man Publishing Company Ltd, 1989) p 27
Sayce, R.U., *Folk-Lore, Folk-Life, Ethnology Folklore*, Vol. 67, No. 2 (London: Taylor & Francis Ltc, 1956), pp. 66–83

The following websites were also used:
boggartholeclough.files.wordpress.com
www.mapit.kk5.org

MAB'S CROSS TALES, WIGAN

Sources:
Harland, John & Wilkinson, T.T. (1873)
Hird, Frank (1912), Volume I, p 167
Landreth, Peter (1841)
Porteus, Revd Thomas Cruddas (1933)
Porteus, Revd Thomas Cruddas (1935)
Roby, John (1872), Volume I
The religious text, 'If any man will come after me…' is from Mark 8:34.

Harland & Wilkinson wrote, in 1873, 'The most ancient and interesting monument in Wigan parish church is placed under the stairs leading to the east gallery where two mangled figures of whitewashed stone preserve the remembrance of Sir William Bradshaigh, of Haigh, and his lady Mabel – he in an antique coat of mail, cross-legged, with his sword partly drawn from the scabbard by his left side, and on his shoulder his shield, charged with two bends; and she in a long robe, veiled, her hands elevated and conjoined in the attitude of fervent prayer.'

The monument has recently been restored and you will now find it in pride of place in the Crawford Chapel.

Mab's Cross still stands on Standishgate. You will find it at the front of Mab's Cross Primary School.

The present Haigh Hall, a country house built between 1827 and 1840, is now a superior events venue, and is worth a visit for its immaculate plasterwork and decoration – and for afternoon tea. The woodwork throughout is an attractively pale smoked oak, and is irreplaceable, as the process in creating it has been lost.

The de Hoghtons of Hoghton Tower

Sources:

Harland, John and Wilkinson, T.T. (1875)

Miller, Geo. C. (1954)

Roby, John (1872), Volume I

We are pleased to acknowledge the help given to us by Sir Bernard de Hoghton, the present baronet. You can enjoy a good day out when you visit historic Hoghton Tower, the de Hoghton's family seat.

Doctor Dee – Walton-le-Dale, Preston

A rather excellent book that details the many times that Satan came to Manchester is:

Vera Winterbottom, *The Devil in Lancashire* (Stockport: The Cloister Press, 1962)

The following websites were also used:

www.mosi.org.uk

www.chethams.org.uk

www.gutenberg.org

The Preston Guild Merchant

Source:

Hird, Frank (1912), Volume II

The Preston Guild Merchant continues to be held every twenty years. Most recently was in 2012, by which time Preston had attained city status, the festivities being carried out with as much pageantry, pomp, popularity, and passion as in 1822, befitting the city's famous motto, 'Proud Preston'!

The Battle of Preston

Sources:

Berry, A.J. (1912)

Clarke, Peter (written 1715) and Paton, Henry M.A. (editor, 1893)

Fishwick, Lieut-Colonel Henry, F.S.A. (1894)

Hird, Frank (1912), Volume I

It is clear from Peter Clarke's contemporary journal that on their march from Kelso the Jacobites behaved with dignity and respect, even towards their opponents, and in the main paid for their lodgings and the goods they acquired on the way.

On the government side, however, he reports bitterly that, after General Wills' men had taken possession of Preston, with force and arms they broke open doors and locks of chambers and closets, and the moneys, plate, goods, and chattels of most inhabitants (who were good subjects to His Majesty's government) they feloniously stole, took, and carried away, contrary to his Majesty's peace, crown, and dignity, and also contrary to the laws of the nation.

TRADITIONS AND SUPERSTITIONS FROM THE FYLDE

The following texts were consulted for these:

Roby, James A., (ed.), *Traditions of Lancashire Past & Present* (Wigan: Owl Books, 1991)

Porter, John, *The History of the Fylde of Lancashire* (Fleetwood & Blackpool: Porter & Sons, 1876)

Finally, the committed and passionate Friends of Real Lancashire have reproduced the Lancashire Proclamation on their website: forl.co.uk/lancashire_day_proclamation.php

LANCASTER – WITCHES AND PERSECUTION

The following books were consulted:

Goodie, Christine, *1612 The Lancashire Witch Trials* (Lancaster: Palatine Books, 2011)

Peel, Edgar, & Southern, Pat, *The Trials of the Lancashire Witches A Study of 17th Century Witchcraft* (Newton Abbot: David and Charles, 1969)

Potts, Thomas, *The Wonderful Discoveries of Witches in the Counties of Lancaster* (London: 1613)

THE DUN COW OF PARLICK, BLEASDALE

Sources:

Grice, Frederick (1953)

Harland, John & Wilkinson, T. T. (1873)

Bleasdale Circle Leaflet, Harris Museum and Art Gallery

Harland & Wilkinson tell us of an old farm at Whittingham, five miles north of Preston, named the 'Old Rib' because, mounted over the door, was the enormous rib of the fabled dun cow.

THE DULE UPO' DUN, CLITHEROE

Source:

Hird, Frank (1912), Volume I, p 215

The biblical quotation is from Luke 15:11–24

LADY SYBIL AND THE MILK-WHITE DOE, SABDEN

Sources:

Grice, Frederick (1953)

Harland, John, & Wilkinson, T.T. (1873)

BIBLIOGRAPHY

Aiken, J., *A Description of the Country from Thirty to Forty Miles Around Manchester* (London: John Stockdale, 1795)

Axon, Ernest (ed), *Bygone Lancashire*, (London: Simpkin, Marshall, Hamilton, Kent & Co. Ltd; Manchester: Brook & Chrystal; Hull: Wh.Liam Andrews & Co., The Hull Press, 1892)

Berry, A.J., *The Story of Preston* (London: Sir Isaac Pitman & Sons Ltd, 1912)

Bleasdale Circle Leaflet (Preston: Harris Museum and Art Gallery)

Bowker, James, *Goblin Tales of Lancashire*, pp 131–9 (in Westwood & Simpson, *Lore of the Land*, p. 401, 1883)

Clarke, Peter, 'A Journall of Severall Occurrences from 2d November 1715, in the Insurrection (began in Scotland) and concluded at Preston in Lancashire, on November 14, MDCCXV', kept by Peter Clarke, being Part I of 'Papers About the Rebellions of 1715 and 1745, Edited from the Original Manuscripts, with Introduction and Notes' (The University Press by T. and A. Constable for the Scottish History Society, written 1715, edited 1893)

Eyre, Kathleen, *Lancashire Ghosts* (Clapham: The Dalesman Publishing Company Ltd, 1989)

Fishwick, Lieut.-Colonel Henry, F.S.A., *A History of Lancashire* (London: Elliot Stock, 1894)

Fishwick, Lieut.-Colonel Henry, F.S.A. and Revd P.H. Ditchfield, M.A.,
    F.S.A. (eds), *Memorials of Old Lancashire (Volumes I and II)* (London:
    Bemrose & Sons Ltd,1909)

Goodie, Christine, *1612 The Lancashire Witch Trials* (Lancaster: Palatine
    Books, 2011)

Grice, Frederick, *Folk Tales of Lancashire* (Thomas Nelson
    and Sons, 1953)

Hardwick, Charles, *On Some Ancient Battle-Fields In Lancashire, and their
    Historical, Legendary, and Aesthetic Association* (Manchester: Abel
    Heywood & Son; London: Simpkin, Marshall, & Co., 1882)

Hardwick, Charles, *Traditions, Superstitions, Folk-Lore, (Chiefly Lancashire
    and the North Of England)* (Manchester: A. Ireland & Co.; London:
    Simpkin, Marshall & Co., 1872)

Harland, John, F.S.A. & T.T. Wilkinson, F.R.A.S. (eds), *Ballads and
    Songs of Lancashire, Collected, Compiled, and Edited, with Notes by John
    Harland*, 2nd ed., corrected, revised, and enlarged by T.T. Wilkinson,
    F.R.A.S. (London: George Routledge and Sons and L.C. Gent, 1875)

Harland, John, F.S.A. & T.T. Wilkinson, F.R.A.S., *Lancashire Legends,
    Traditions, Pageants, Sports, etc.* (London: George Routledge and Sons;
    Manchester: L.C. Gent, 1873)

Harland, John, F.S.A. & T.T. Wilkinson, F.R.A.S. (eds), *Lancashire Folk-Lore,
    Illustrative of the Superstitious Beliefs and Practices, Local Customs and Usages
    of the People of the County Palatine* (Covent Garden: Frederick Warne
    and Co.; New York: Scribner and Co.; London: Savill and Edwards,1867)

Hird, Frank, *Lancashire Stories, Volumes I & II, Containing All that Appeals
    to the Heart and the Imagination in the Lancashire of Today and of Many
    Yesterdays* (London and Edinburgh: T.C. and E.C. Jack, 1912)

Landreth, Peter, *Legends of Lancashire* (London: Simpkin, Marshall, &
    Co., 1841)

Ludlam, Harry, *The Mummy of Birchen Bower* (Slough: W. Foulsham &
    Co. Ltd, 1966)

Miller, Geo. C. (with forward by the present Baronet, Cuthbert
    de Hoghton, Bart.), *Hoghton Tower in History and Romance*, (Preston:
    The Guardian Press, 1954)

Palmer, John, *History of the Siege of Manchester by the King's Forces Under
    the Command of Lord Strange 1642* (Manchester: John Leigh, 1822)

Peel, Edgar & Pat Southern, *The Trials of the Lancashire Witches A Study of 17th Century Witchcraft* (Newton Abbot: David and Charles, 1969)

Porter, John, *The History of the Fylde of Lancashire* (Fleetwood and Blackpool: W. Porter & Sons, 1876)

Porteus, Revd Thomas Cruddas, *Legend of Mab's Cross* (R. Platt Ltd,1933) (Note: The books about Mab's Cross by Revd Porteus are available in the Reference Section of the Museum of Wigan Life, Library Street)

Porteus, Revd Thomas Cruddas, *New Light on the Mab's Cross Legend* (Thos. Wall & Sons Ltd, *Observer* Office, 1935)

Potts, Thomas, *The Wonderful Discoveries of Witches in the Counties of Lancaster* (London: 1613)

Robinson, Cedric & Olive Robinson, *Sand Pilot of Morecambe Bay* (Atlantic Transport Publishers, 1998)

Roby, James A. (ed.), *Traditions of Lancashire Past & Present* (Wigan: Owl Books, 1991)

Roby, John, M.R.S.L., *Traditions Of Lancashire, Volumes I & II, Fifth Edition* (London: George Routledge and Sons; Manchester: L.C. Gent, 1872)

Sayce, R.U., *Folk-Lore, Folk-Life, Ethnology Folklore, Vol. 67, No. 2* pp. 66–83 (Taylor & Francis Ltd, 1956)

Winterbottom, Vera, *The Devil in Lancashire* (Stockport: The Cloister Press, 1962)

Wood, J., *The Story of Manchester* (London: T. Werner Laurie Ltd, 1915)

Woods, Albert, A.R.C.A. (painted), Bruton, F.A., M.A., Litt.D. (described), *Lancashire* (London: A. & C. Black Ltd, 1921)